CONTENTS

ACCEPTING
THE CHALLENGE

Congratulations! You are on your way to taking your faith to the next level. This *Activated Disciple 40-Day Challenge Journal* will help you move from simply believing and practicing your faith to radically living it.

Every day is a new opportunity to walk with Jesus and discover aspects of him and yourself that you would not otherwise come to know. Fully participating in your relationship with Jesus will truly make a difference in your life, assuring both growth and fruitfulness.

This journal is a tool to keep you focused for forty days on the One who will bring about the transformation you really desire. Change in your life, whether it be growing in virtue, stopping bad habits from flourishing, or gaining wisdom for life's many decisions, comes from repeatedly meeting Christ, the source of infinite love, wisdom, and protection.

The goal of this forty-day challenge is ultimately to make walking with Jesus a habit, a part of who you are. In the end, I hope you say, "I can't live without it and didn't know what I was missing." Many people say they need to spend more time praying, reading the Bible, and looking for opportunities to be a witness for Christ. Unfortunately, the desire to do more is not often met with a structure that lends itself to a habit-forming exercise. My hope is that *The Activated Disciple 40-Day Challenge Journal* will help you make meeting Jesus multiple times a day a new habit in your life.

Before you begin the forty-day challenge, be sure to read *The Activated Disciple: Taking Your Faith to the Next Level*, by Jeff Cavins

(Ascension, 2018), as much of what you will be doing in these next forty days flows from the pages of that book.

DAILY PRACTICE

Before I explain the flow of each day of this challenge, I would like to make a couple of key points that will correctly orient you as a disciple to the Lord:

- It is important to remind yourself every day during this journey that you are responding to an invitation from the Lord to become his disciple. He chose you and has invited you to follow him and become like him. This exercise is not another invitation to simply learn more; it is an invitation to grow, to change, to be transformed by knowing Christ's mind, heart, and plans. As you come to understand the mind of Christ and have a grasp of his plan for humanity, you will be compelled to continue his mission by actively looking for opportunities to express it publicly with friends and family.

- I encourage you to come up with daily signposts that will remind you that you are actively following, all through the day, the second Person of the Trinity. By signposts, I mean things like hearing a certain alert on your smartphone or seeing a particular color of car. Every time you notice a signpost, pause and remind yourself that you are on a journey with Jesus every moment of the day. Give yourself every opportunity to be deliberate about your responsibilities as a disciple.

- Pray that your walk with Christ will always be in your thoughts and that every encounter will be influenced by the one you are walking with: Jesus.

The forty-day challenge is designed to enable you to reconfigure your life as a disciple of Jesus by focusing on eight virtues that will bring about change in your heart. As you work through the exercises each day, you will be crafting the lifestyle of a disciple.

The eight virtues are:

1. **Love**
2. **Forgiveness**
3. **Humility**
4. **Patience**
5. **Selflessness**
6. **Kindness**
7. **Attentiveness**
8. **Contrition**

As you steep your heart and mind in these virtues (for five days each), you will grow and become more and more like Jesus. For each virtue, I have created two inspirational videos. I suggest you watch the first one on the day you begin the virtue, complete two days of the challenge on that virtue, and watch the second video on the third day. This journal contains a checkbox on those days to prompt you to watch the videos. If you are doing the forty-day challenge with a group, you may want to watch the videos again together (as a review) prior to your small-group discussion. The videos are available at ascensionpress.com.

Each day of the challenge is structured into four parts: (1) A Word with God, (2) Situational Awareness, (3) Check-In, and (4) The Shape of My Day. Participating in Mass regularly, going to confession, praying the Rosary, and being involved in Bible study are all basic disciplines of the disciple, so adding these to your days is also encouraged.

PART 1: **A WORD WITH GOD** – *Lectio Divina*

Each and every day, the activated disciple must spend time with the Lord in prayer. This is the foundation of your relationship and must be given prime time and attention. I suggest meeting with the Lord for fifteen to twenty minutes each morning to do *lectio divina* with the text given in this journal for that day. Remember, consistency in time and place will better assure your success in developing the habit.

In chapter 6 of *The Activated Disciple: Taking Your Faith to the Next Level*, you will find a description of the steps of *lectio divina—lectio, meditatio, oratio,* and *contemplatio—*along with an example for each. Like my friend and colleague Dr. Tim Gray, I also introduce a fifth step, which Dr. Gray calls *operatio* but for the challenge I call *imitatio* (imitate). The fifth step will give you a chance to practice a specific attitude or action of a disciple each day.

In your time of *lectio,* you will be listening to what the Lord is saying to you that day. You will have the opportunity to talk to the Lord and bring your concerns to him, and he will be able to point out to you what he wants you to focus on that day. Make sure to write down your thoughts and what you believe God is pointing out to you. Taking what God reveals to you in prayer into your day will be very helpful in your growth, and it may become just what your friends and family need to hear from you.

PART 2: **SITUATIONAL AWARENESS**

Be aware of your surroundings. Look for opportunities not only to grow in the virtues but also to express them in your encounters throughout each day. As you go about your day, be aware of opportunities to apply what you gained in your prayer time with the Lord. I have always been amazed at how many times the nuggets of truth the Lord has revealed to me in prayer become vital throughout the day.

Be vigilant, awake, and conscious of the fact that you are a representative of the Lord and will have opportunities to continue his mission. At some time during the day, take a few moments to write down your observations, conversations, or anything else that you feel was important that came from your time of prayer. The more you do this, the more you will see what God is revealing to you.

It is during your day that you can bring in other types of devotions, such as the Divine Mercy Chaplet, Bible study, or the Rosary.

Begin to develop a pattern—a rhythm to your life that continuously draws you close to the Lord.

PART 3: **CHECK-IN**

It is essential to surround yourself with the saints who are related to the most important tasks in your life. I call this chosen group *my posse,* and being aware of my relationship with them throughout the day has added a refreshing dimension to my walk with Jesus. This will happen for you too. Your friendship with the saints will help to keep you in line with God's will for your life by providing examples of how to live, as well as needed prayer support. Since we cannot get to know all the saints, I would encourage you to bring together about five saints you can call upon during the day. You can collect their writings or their biographies, which will deepen your relationship with them. This exercise has been a source of strength for me personally.

In addition to your relationship with the saints, you are also in relationship with the body of Christ here on earth. Walking as activated disciples is not something we do alone; instead, we walk as a family, the body of Christ. Choose someone in your life you can check in with weekly to share how your walk with Christ is going. The person you pick should be someone you can depend on, someone who will advise you wisely and pray for you faithfully. This person will be your *accountability partner* throughout the challenge.

PART 4: **THE SHAPE OF MY DAY**

It is important to remember that the shape of your day is the result of intentional decisions to follow Christ and grow as a disciple. The shape of your day begins with the shape of your morning and your decision to meet with Jesus, and continues with carrying that meeting into your afternoon and reviewing your day in the evening. There is a shape to your day as a disciple, a shape that reflects the fact that you are in love with Jesus and actively pursuing him.

Throughout your day, you will experience many situations, persons, problems, and opportunities. You will review them using the Examen prayer from St. Ignatius' Spiritual Exercises. The Examen is a simple but powerful prayer that takes just a few minutes at the end of the day. To pray it, you will put yourself in the Lord's presence and then review and evaluate, with him, how your day went. Were you aware throughout the day of what God revealed to you in prayer? If not, why not? What do you need to change tomorrow to help build this habit of a disciple?

The purpose of this time with the Lord is to contemplate those things you did well, the victories, and also the areas that need correction. This is the time in your day when as a disciple you can rejoice in the great things the Lord is accomplishing in your life and can notice negative patterns that are beginning to develop. Dealing quickly with patterns that could pose a problem in your walk with the Lord is very important, and keeping to your set schedule will help you do this.

At the end of the day, you can write down any great points of growth and those things that you want to focus on tomorrow. Remember, you are in the process of growth, so don't be too hard on yourself. Becoming like Jesus is a process, but one worth the effort.

YOU ARE PART OF A MOVEMENT

Using *The Activated Disciple 40-Day Challenge Journal* is not just an individual endeavor. Thousands of others are making this walk with you. Many parishes are taking the forty-day challenge together and are meeting to compare notes and share stories.

Thank you for taking this challenge! Becoming an activated disciple will not only change your life—it will change the world. We are not going to change the world by just teaching the Faith; we must put it into practice, and each person must see himself or herself as a representative bringing all that Christ taught and did into the world. Continue to walk in the power of your confirmation and the graces you received at Baptism.

PRE-CHALLENGE ASSESSMENT

Measuring your growth as a disciple is important. Before beginning this forty-day challenge, take a moment to think about the following questions.

1. **How would you describe your life as a disciple?** Use the space below to honestly reflect on your current relationship with Jesus.

_____

_____

_____

_____

_____

_____

2. **After completing this challenge, where do you hope to be as a disciple?**

_____

_____

_____

_____

_____

_____

_____

PREPARING FOR YOUR
FORTY-DAY CHALLENGE

1. **Watch the introductory video.** Jot down anything that resonates with you. *Videos are available at ascensionpress.com*

_____

_____

_____

_____

_____

_____

2. **Assemble your posse.** List saints who will accompany you, inspire you, and pray for you during this forty-day challenge.

_____

_____

_____

_____

_____

_____

_____

_____

3. **Choose your accountability partner.** Pick someone to check in with weekly. Write down their name and contact information.

Name: _____

Contact Info: _____

4. **Set your schedule.** Schedule a daily time for your "Word with God" (*lectio divina*), "Check-In" (with your posse of saints), and reflection on "The Shape of My Day" (the Examen prayer). Include ways to remind yourself to adhere to your schedule—perhaps a calendar reminder, an alarm on your phone or watch, or a note on your bathroom mirror.

A Word with God (*lectio divina*). Make this prayer time special. Having your Bible, this journal, a notebook, and a candle or other special item in your prayer space can enhance your prayer time.

Time: _____

Location: _____

Special items: _____

Check-In. Set a plan to call on your posse as well as your accountability partner.

When I will call on my posse: You can invoke your saints all at one time, at various times throughout the day, or in various circumstances. Or you can lean on one saint each day or one saint for each virtue. It is up to you.

Times: _____

When I will call on my accountability partner: Write down the day and time you plan to connect each week.

Day: _____

Time: _____

The Shape of My Day. Take time to reflect on the question, "Did the shape of my day reflect that I am in love with Christ?" Use the Examen prayer to review your day. It is good to get in the habit of doing this before going to bed.

When I will review my day: _____

NOTES

" We become what we love, and who we love shapes what we become. If we love things, we become a thing. If we love nothing, we become nothing. Imitation is not a literal mimicking of Christ; rather, it means becoming the image of the beloved, an image disclosed through transformation. ... This means we are to become vessels of God's compassionate love for others. "

— *St. Clare of Assisi on contemplation,
as described by Ilia Delio*
(Franciscan Prayer, 2004)

LOVE

If your family or friends were asked how they knew that you were a disciple of Jesus, what would they say?

After the Lord called twelve men to become his disciples, he trained them and sent them out to do the work of his kingdom. But how did others know that these men were disciples of Jesus? Was it evident in the way they spoke, in what they wore? Did their political views or those with whom they associated reveal the One they were following?

There are many ways the public could identify these men as followers of Jesus, but he established one criterion by which all could identify his followers. Jesus said, "By this all men will know that you are my disciples, if you have love for one another" (John 13:35).

Every day we are given opportunities to show the world who God is by loving others. This great opportunity demands that we respond to relationships differently than the world does. Love is not merely an emotional feeling of affection but a power that heals wounds, overcomes prejudices, and renews relationships. Love is a profound and life-changing power that comes from God to the world through the heart of a disciple. What is distinct about the love of God is that it is not initiated or executed by mere emotions.

The Greek verb *phileo* speaks of friendship or affection for someone. This kind of love may bring people together in a shared activity that results in a bond. *Phileo* is based on feelings and often prompted by emotions. The Greek verb *agape* is different from *phileo,* in that it speaks of unselfish and unconditional love that wills the good of another. *Agape* is often described as the kind of

love God demonstrates. The concept of *agape* is used to describe the attitude of God toward his Son (John 17:26), the human race (John 3:16), and those who obey Jesus (John 14:21).

The clear distinction between the two concepts of love is seen in the daily application. Since love as an emotion is prompted by feelings, it cannot be commanded; *phileo* cannot be forced and may not be used in a command to love.

In contrast, *agape* love, which is the most self-sacrificing love there is, may be commanded; hence, Jesus commanded his disciples to *"love [agape] your enemies"* (Matthew 5:44).

The mandate for Christians to love our enemies stretches our natural capacity to love to a supernatural capacity that changes the world. God bestows his love and mercy on those who are undeserving of it, and we in turn extend God's love toward others. It is the love of God flowing through you that will penetrate hardened hearts and attract others to God. This week, look for opportunities to freely give of yourself, keeping in mind the eternal good of others.

TALMIDIM CHALLENGE

In the first century, disciples were called *talmidim*. A *talmid* (disciple) was someone who was completely in agreement with his rabbi's worldview and wanted to learn it and live it. Below are some challenges to help you become a disciple of Jesus, the ultimate rabbi.

- Make the choice to love someone. Look for opportunities to love from your will rather than from emotion.

- Take opportunities to love where you will not necessarily be repaid.

- Notice others who are loving you. Take a moment to thank them.

DAY 1
ACTIVATING LOVE

☐ Watch video: Love, Part 1

A Word with God – *Lectio Divina*

LECTIO
(READ)

Read **1 Corinthians 13:4-13** slowly, then read it again. Read it a third time. Look for details. Notice key words, verbs and nouns, and anything repeated, compared, or contrasted.

MEDITATIO
(MEDITATE)

Mentally "chew" on the passage's key words or images to extract their meaning. Let the words sink in and take hold. What words or phrases catch and hold your attention?

_____

_____

_____

_____

_____

_____

_____

ORATIO
(PRAY)

Pay attention to the way your meditation connects with your life, and respond to what you find. This is your time to "have a word" with God through his Word! Speak to him in your words. Make it personal. Share your heart: He is listening.

CONTEMPLATIO
(CONTEMPLATE)

Savor being in God's presence. Enjoy what God has given you.

IMITATIO
(IMITATE)

Resolve to act on what God has revealed to you in *lectio divina*. Recall the characteristics of a disciple at the focus of today's Scripture verses. What specific attitude or action of a disciple will you imitate?

_____

_____

_____

_____

_____

_____

_____

A WORD OF ENCOURAGEMENT

"It is interesting that St. Paul draws a correlation between walking in love and maturity. When we walk in love, we leave our childish ways and respond to people as Christ would."

— *Jeff Cavins*

Situational Awareness

Note circumstances during your day that gave you the opportunity to exercise the characteristic of a disciple that God revealed to you in your time with him.

_____

_____

_____

_____

_____

_____

_____

_____

_____

_____

Check-In

Cultivate your ongoing relationship with your saintly posse daily, and work with your accountability partner once a week to discuss your walk with Christ.

☐ Today I checked in with my posse.

☐ Today I checked in with my accountability partner.

The Shape of My Day

1. Express Gratitude: Give thanks to God for the gifts he has given you today.

Today I give thanks for _____

_____

_____

_____

2. Seek Grace: Ask God for the insight to see what he's been trying to reveal to you throughout the day, and for guidance in recognizing the hurdles you faced in trying to do his will.

Lord, grant me the grace today to _____

_____

_____

_____

3. Review the Day: Review the day you just lived like a film in your head, paying close attention to moments you felt close to God, those in which you did not, and how you chose to respond in these moments. Then talk to the Lord; share your heart.

Lord, I felt close to you today when _____

_____

_____

_____

4. **Ask for Forgiveness:** Admit any mistakes you made today and ask God to heal your heart.

Today, Lord, I ask forgiveness for _____

_____

_____

_____

_____

5. **Look Forward:** Take the insights God has given you today and ask him where he is leading you. What does he want from you tomorrow? Together, in relationship with him and through his grace, prepare yourself to take on the next day.

Today I experienced _____

_____

_____

_____

Tomorrow I am going to focus on _____

_____

_____

_____

_____

☐ *I Lived Day 1 as an Activated Disciple!*

DAY 2

ACTIVATING LOVE

A Word with God – *Lectio Divina*

LECTIO
(READ)

Read **1 John 4:7-12** slowly, then read it again. Read it a third time. Look for details. Notice key words, verbs and nouns, and anything repeated, compared, or contrasted.

MEDITATIO
(MEDITATE)

Mentally "chew" on the passage's key words or images to extract their meaning. Let the words sink in and take hold. What words or phrases catch and hold your attention?

_____

_____

_____

_____

_____

_____

_____

ORATIO
(PRAY)

Pay attention to the way your meditation connects with your life, and respond to what you find. This is your time to "have a word" with God through his Word! Speak to him in your words. Make it personal. Share your heart: He is listening.

CONTEMPLATIO
(CONTEMPLATE)

Savor being in God's presence. Enjoy what God has given you.

IMITATIO
(IMITATE)

Resolve to act on what God has revealed to you in *lectio divina*. Recall the characteristics of a disciple at the focus of today's Scripture verses. What specific attitude or action of a disciple will you imitate?

_____

_____

_____

_____

_____

_____

A WORD OF ENCOURAGEMENT

"Throughout the day, contemplate God's love for you,
and see if your love for others grows in proportion
to your understanding of how God loves you."

— *Jeff Cavins*

Situational Awareness

Note circumstances during your day that gave you the opportunity to exercise the characteristic of a disciple that God revealed to you in your time with him.

_____

_____

_____

_____

_____

_____

_____

_____

_____

_____

_____

Check-In

Cultivate your ongoing relationship with your saintly posse daily, and work with your accountability partner once a week to discuss your walk with Christ.

☐ Today I checked in with my posse

☐ Today I checked in with my accountability partner.

The Shape of My Day

1. Express Gratitude: Give thanks to God for the gifts he has given you today.

Today I give thanks for _____

_____

_____

_____

2. Seek Grace: Ask God for the insight to see what he's been trying to reveal to you throughout the day, and for guidance in recognizing the hurdles you faced in trying to do his will.

Lord, grant me the grace today to _____

_____

_____

_____

_____

3. Review the Day: Review the day you just lived like a film in your head, paying close attention to moments you felt close to God, those in which you did not, and how you chose to respond in these moments. Then talk to the Lord; share your heart.

Lord, I felt close to you today when _____

_____

_____

_____

_____

4. Ask for Forgiveness: Admit any mistakes you made today and ask God to heal your heart.

Today, Lord, I ask forgiveness for _____

_____

_____

_____

_____

5. Look Forward: Take the insights God has given you today and ask him where he is leading you. What does he want from you tomorrow? Together, in relationship with him and through his grace, prepare yourself to take on the next day.

Today I experienced _____

_____

_____

_____

Tomorrow I am going to focus on _____

_____

_____

_____

_____

☐ *I Lived Day 2 as an Activated Disciple!*

DAY 3

ACTIVATING LOVE

☐ Watch video: Love, Part 2

A Word with God – *Lectio Divina*

LECTIO
(READ)

Read **Ephesians 5:1-4** slowly, then read it again. Read it a third time. Look for details. Notice key words, verbs and nouns, and anything repeated, compared, or contrasted.

MEDITATIO
(MEDITATE)

Mentally "chew" on the passage's key words or images to extract their meaning. Let the words sink in and take hold. What words or phrases catch and hold your attention?

_____

_____

_____

_____

_____

_____

_____

ORATIO
(PRAY)

Pay attention to the way your meditation connects with your life, and respond to what you find. This is your time to "have a word" with God through his Word! Speak to him in your words. Make it personal. Share your heart: He is listening.

CONTEMPLATIO
(CONTEMPLATE)

Savor being in God's presence. Enjoy what God has given you.

IMITATIO
(IMITATE)

Resolve to act on what God has revealed to you in *lectio divina*. Recall the characteristics of a disciple at the focus of today's Scripture verses. What specific attitude or action of a disciple will you imitate?

_____

_____

_____

_____

_____

_____

A WORD OF ENCOURAGEMENT

"Be aware of the moments when things might not go your way.
You may not be treated the way you think you should. It's OK. It will
be an opportunity to imitate God and love as Christ loves you."

— *Jeff Cavins*

Situational Awareness

Note circumstances during your day that gave you the opportunity to exercise the characteristic of a disciple that God revealed to you in your time with him.

_____

_____

_____

_____

_____

_____

_____

_____

_____

_____

Check-In

Cultivate your ongoing relationship with your saintly posse daily, and work with your accountability partner once a week to discuss your walk with Christ.

☐ Today I checked in with my posse.

☐ Today I checked in with my accountability partner.

The Shape of My Day

1. Express Gratitude: Give thanks to God for the gifts he has given you today.

Today I give thanks for _____

_____

_____

_____

2. Seek Grace: Ask God for the insight to see what he's been trying to reveal to you throughout the day, and for guidance in recognizing the hurdles you faced in trying to do his will.

Lord, grant me the grace today to _____

_____

_____

_____

3. Review the Day: Review the day you just lived like a film in your head, paying close attention to moments you felt close to God, those in which you did not, and how you chose to respond in these moments. Then talk to the Lord; share your heart.

Lord, I felt close to you today when _____

_____

_____

_____

4. Ask for Forgiveness: Admit any mistakes you made today and ask God to heal your heart.

Today, Lord, I ask forgiveness for _____

_____

_____

_____

5. Look Forward: Take the insights God has given you today and ask him where he is leading you. What does he want from you tomorrow? Together, in relationship with him and through his grace, prepare yourself to take on the next day.

Today I experienced _____

_____

_____

_____

Tomorrow I am going to focus on _____

_____

_____

_____

☐ *I Lived Day 3 as an Activated Disciple!*

DAY 4
ACTIVATING LOVE

A Word with God – *Lectio Divina*

LECTIO
(READ)

Read **Mark 12:28-34** slowly, then read it again. Read it a third time. Look for details. Notice key words, verbs and nouns, and anything repeated, compared, or contrasted.

MEDITATIO
(MEDITATE)

Mentally "chew" on the passage's key words or images to extract their meaning. Let the words sink in and take hold. What words or phrases catch and hold your attention?

_____

_____

_____

_____

_____

_____

_____

ORATIO
(PRAY)

Pay attention to the way your meditation connects with your life, and respond to what you find. This is your time to "have a word" with God through his Word! Speak to him in your words. Make it personal. Share your heart: He is listening.

CONTEMPLATIO
(CONTEMPLATE)

Savor being in God's presence. Enjoy what God has given you.

IMITATIO
(IMITATE)

Resolve to act on what God has revealed to you in *lectio divina.* Recall the characteristics of a disciple at the focus of today's Scripture verses. What specific attitude or action of a disciple will you imitate?

_____

_____

_____

_____

_____

_____

A WORD OF ENCOURAGEMENT
"I encourage you to take part in a small experiment today.
Love your family and the people you meet today the way you would
want to be loved. The opportunities are there if you look for them."

— *Jeff Cavins*

Situational Awareness

Note circumstances during your day that gave you the opportunity to exercise the characteristic of a disciple that God revealed to you in your time with him.

_____

_____

_____

_____

_____

_____

_____

_____

_____

_____

_____

Check-In

Cultivate your ongoing relationship with your saintly posse daily, and work with your accountability partner once a week to discuss your walk with Christ.

☐ Today I checked in with my posse.

☐ Today I checked in with my accountability partner.

The Shape of My Day

1. **Express Gratitude:** Give thanks to God for the gifts he has given you today.

   Today I give thanks for _____

   _____

   _____

   _____

2. **Seek Grace:** Ask God for the insight to see what he's been trying to reveal to you throughout the day, and for guidance in recognizing the hurdles you faced in trying to do his will.

   Lord, grant me the grace today to _____

   _____

   _____

   _____

   _____

3. **Review the Day:** Review the day you just lived like a film in your head, paying close attention to moments you felt close to God, those in which you did not, and how you chose to respond in these moments. Then talk to the Lord; share your heart.

   Lord, I felt close to you today when _____

   _____

   _____

   _____

   _____

4. Ask for Forgiveness: Admit any mistakes you made today and ask God to heal your heart.

Today, Lord, I ask forgiveness for _____

_____

_____

_____

5. Look Forward: Take the insights God has given you today and ask him where he is leading you. What does he want from you tomorrow? Together, in relationship with him and through his grace, prepare yourself to take on the next day.

Today I experienced _____

_____

_____

_____

Tomorrow I am going to focus on _____

_____

_____

_____

☐ *I Lived Day 4 as an Activated Disciple!*

DAY 5
ACTIVATING LOVE

A Word with God – *Lectio Divina*

LECTIO
(READ)

Read **Matthew 5:43-48** slowly, then read it again. Read it a third time. Look for details. Notice key words, verbs and nouns, and anything repeated, compared, or contrasted.

MEDITATIO
(MEDITATE)

Mentally "chew" on the passage's key words or images to extract their meaning. Let the words sink in and take hold. What words or phrases catch and hold your attention?

_____

_____

_____

_____

_____

_____

_____

ORATIO
(PRAY)

Pay attention to the way your meditation connects with your life, and respond to what you find. This is your time to "have a word" with God through his Word! Speak to him in your words. Make it personal. Share your heart: He is listening.

CONTEMPLATIO
(CONTEMPLATE)

Savor being in God's presence. Enjoy what God has given you.

IMITATIO
(IMITATE)

Resolve to act on what God has revealed to you in *lectio divina*. Recall the characteristics of a disciple at the focus of today's Scripture verses. What specific attitude or action of a disciple will you imitate?

_____

_____

_____

_____

_____

_____

_____

A WORD OF ENCOURAGEMENT

"You may be tempted to only engage with those who are like you and share common interests. Make a point to reach out to someone who may not have shown you kindness in the last few days or weeks."

— *Jeff Cavins*

Situational Awareness

Note circumstances during your day that gave you the opportunity to exercise the characteristic of a disciple that God revealed to you in your time with him.

_____

_____

_____

_____

_____

_____

_____

_____

_____

_____

Check-In

Cultivate your ongoing relationship with your saintly posse daily, and work with your accountability partner once a week to discuss your walk with Christ.

☐ Today I checked in with my posse.

☐ Today I checked in with my accountability partner.

The Shape of My Day

1. Express Gratitude: Give thanks to God for the gifts he has given you today.

Today I give thanks for _____

_____

_____

_____

2. Seek Grace: Ask God for the insight to see what he's been trying to reveal to you throughout the day, and for guidance in recognizing the hurdles you faced in trying to do his will.

Lord, grant me the grace today to _____

_____

_____

_____

_____

3. Review the Day: Review the day you just lived like a film in your head, paying close attention to moments you felt close to God, those in which you did not, and how you chose to respond in these moments. Then talk to the Lord; share your heart.

Lord, I felt close to you today when _____

_____

_____

_____

_____

4. Ask for Forgiveness: Admit any mistakes you made today and ask God to heal your heart.

Today, Lord, I ask forgiveness for _____

_____

_____

_____

_____

5. Look Forward: Take the insights God has given you today and ask him where he is leading you. What does he want from you tomorrow? Together, in relationship with him and through his grace, prepare yourself to take on the next day.

Today I experienced _____

_____

_____

_____

Tomorrow I am going to focus on _____

_____

_____

_____

☐ *I Lived Day 5 as an Activated Disciple!*

" During mental prayer, it is well, at times, to imagine that many insults and injuries are being heaped upon us, that misfortunes have befallen us, and then strive to train our heart to bear and forgive these things patiently, in imitation of our Savior. This is the way to acquire a strong spirit. "

— *St. Philip Neri*

FORGIVENESS

What is the hardest part of being a disciple of Christ? The hardest part for us was also the hardest part for Jesus: picking up our cross and forgiving the trespasses of others. Yet forgiving others leads to freedom, both for you and for the one you are forgiving.

It is very important for you, as an activated disciple, to understand that in this world you are going to have difficulties and tribulations. The good news is that Jesus has overcome the world, but at a cost: the Cross. The greatest expression of love in world history was Jesus' cross, the place where sin was forgiven—where humanity was released from the chains and eternal consequences of sin and set free.

Several words come to mind when we contemplate Christ's cross—*will, love, agony, reconciliation.* We would do well to pay attention to these words in our daily lives, as we are each called to pick up our cross and continue carrying out his ministry of reconciliation.

WILL

Jesus didn't have to forgive us—he willed to forgive us and face the pain of the Cross. We too must exercise our will if we are going to walk in forgiveness. We don't forgive others because we feel like it; we forgive because it is what we are called to do as followers of Christ. Forgiveness flows from the heart through an act of the will, releasing those who have hurt us without any expectation of goodwill on their part.

LOVE

Jesus loved us with a love that considered our eternal good. He didn't love us just to become friends or because he felt moved by our bleak condition. He wanted us to spend eternity with him in heaven; therefore, he loved us with a total gift of self. We too are called to forgive others with their eternal good in mind. This is what will distinguish us in the world today. To love your friends and family is expected, but to love your enemy and those who have hurt you is to draw from the love of the Trinity.

AGONY

One word that describes forgiveness is *agony*. From the agony of the garden to the agony of the Cross, Jesus embraced his suffering for us. As a disciple of Christ, you too will experience an agony in the midst of releasing others. This goes with the territory of a disciple and must be embraced and offered up in union with Christ's suffering. This is what the Apostle Paul meant when he said, "Now I rejoice in my sufferings for your sake, and in my flesh I complete what is lacking in Christ's afflictions for the sake of his body, that is, the Church" (Colossians 1:24).

RECONCILIATION

As disciples, we have been given the ministry of reconciliation. This means that we are tasked with the mission of bringing people together with Jesus in the hope that they will become members of the household of God, the Church. This means that we see people differently now that we are disciples. St. Paul said,

> Therefore, if any one is in Christ, he is a new creation; the old has passed away, behold, the new has come. All this is from God, who through Christ reconciled us to himself and gave us the ministry of reconciliation; that is, in Christ God was reconciling the world to himself, not counting their trespasses against them, and entrusting to us the message of reconciliation. So we are ambassadors for Christ, God making his appeal through us. We beg you on behalf of Christ, be reconciled to God. (2 Corinthians 5:17-20)

TALMIDIM CHALLENGE

- Take a moment in prayer and ask the Lord if there is anyone you are failing to forgive in your life. Make sure that you bring this up the next time you go to confession.

- Meditate on how the Lord forgave you on the Cross, and pray that your heart toward others reflects his heart toward you.

- Resolve in your heart and mind that you are not going to fall into the trap of unforgiveness when you are hurt by others.

DAY 6

ACTIVATING
FORGIVENESS

☐ Watch video: Forgiveness, Part 1

A Word with God – *Lectio Divina*

LECTIO
(READ)

Read **Luke 17:1-4** slowly, then read it again. Read it a third time. Look for details. Notice key words, verbs and nouns, and anything repeated, compared, or contrasted.

MEDITATIO
(MEDITATE)

Mentally "chew" on the passage's key words or images to extract their meaning. Let the words sink in and take hold. What words or phrases catch and hold your attention?

_____

_____

_____

_____

_____

_____

_____

_____

ORATIO
(PRAY)

Pay attention to the way your meditation connects with your life, and respond to what you find. This is your time to "have a word" with God through his Word! Speak to him in your words. Make it personal. Share your heart: He is listening.

CONTEMPLATIO
(CONTEMPLATE)

Savor being in God's presence. Enjoy what God has given you.

IMITATIO
(IMITATE)

Resolve to act on what God has revealed to you in *lectio divina*. Recall the characteristics of a disciple at the focus of today's Scripture verses. What specific attitude or action of a disciple will you imitate?

_____

_____

_____

_____

_____

_____

A WORD OF ENCOURAGEMENT

"Begin today with the attitude that if anyone offends you or hurts you in any way, you are going to forgive them even up to seven times. This will help you to see how much Christ loves them ... and you!"

— *Jeff Cavins*

Situational Awareness

Note circumstances during your day that gave you the opportunity to exercise the characteristic of a disciple that God revealed to you in your time with him.

_____

_____

_____

_____

_____

_____

_____

_____

_____

_____

_____

Check-In

Cultivate your ongoing relationship with your saintly posse daily, and work with your accountability partner once a week to discuss your walk with Christ.

☐ Today I checked in with my posse.

☐ Today I checked in with my accountability partner.

The Shape of My Day

1. Express Gratitude: Give thanks to God for the gifts he has given you today.

Today I give thanks for _____

_____

_____

_____

2. Seek Grace: Ask God for the insight to see what he's been trying to reveal to you throughout the day, and for guidance in recognizing the hurdles you faced in trying to do his will.

Lord, grant me the grace today to _____

_____

_____

_____

3. Review the Day: Review the day you just lived like a film in your head, paying close attention to moments you felt close to God, those in which you did not, and how you chose to respond in these moments. Then talk to the Lord; share your heart.

Lord, I felt close to you today when _____

_____

_____

_____

4. **Ask for Forgiveness:** Admit any mistakes you made today and ask God to heal your heart.

Today, Lord, I ask forgiveness for _____

_____

_____

_____

_____

5. **Look Forward:** Take the insights God has given you today and ask him where he is leading you. What does he want from you tomorrow? Together, in relationship with him and through his grace, prepare yourself to take on the next day.

Today I experienced _____

_____

_____

_____

Tomorrow I am going to focus on _____

_____

_____

_____

☐ *I Lived Day 6 as an Activated Disciple!*

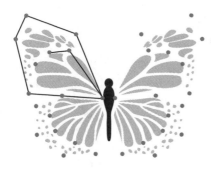

DAY 7
ACTIVATING FORGIVENESS

A Word with God – *Lectio Divina*

LECTIO
(READ)

Read **Matthew 26:26-29** slowly, then read it again. Read it a third time. Look for details. Notice key words, verbs and nouns, and anything repeated, compared, or contrasted.

MEDITATIO
(MEDITATE)

Mentally "chew" on the passage's key words or images to extract their meaning. Let the words sink in and take hold. What words or phrases catch and hold your attention?

_____

_____

_____

_____

_____

_____

_____

ORATIO
(PRAY)

Pay attention to the way your meditation connects with your life, and respond to what you find. This is your time to "have a word" with God through his Word! Speak to him in your words. Make it personal. Share your heart: He is listening.

CONTEMPLATIO
(CONTEMPLATE)

Savor being in God's presence. Enjoy what God has given you.

IMITATIO
(IMITATE)

Resolve to act on what God has revealed to you in *lectio divina*. Recall the characteristics of a disciple at the focus of today's Scripture verses. What specific attitude or action of a disciple will you imitate?

_____

_____

_____

_____

_____

_____

A WORD OF ENCOURAGEMENT

"The color red reminds us of the blood of Christ. Jesus' sacrifice for us results in the forgiveness of sins. Throughout today, when you see the color red, offer up a quick prayer of thanks to God and remind yourself that you too are a forgiving person."

— *Jeff Cavins*

Situational Awareness

Note circumstances during your day that gave you the opportunity to exercise the characteristic of a disciple that God revealed to you in your time with him.

_____

_____

_____

_____

_____

_____

_____

_____

_____

_____

Check-In

Cultivate your ongoing relationship with your saintly posse daily, and work with your accountability partner once a week to discuss your walk with Christ.

☐ Today I checked in with my posse.

☐ Today I checked in with my accountability partner.

The Shape of My Day

1. Express Gratitude: Give thanks to God for the gifts he has given you today.

Today I give thanks for _____

_____

_____

_____

2. Seek Grace: Ask God for the insight to see what he's been trying to reveal to you throughout the day, and for guidance in recognizing the hurdles you faced in trying to do his will.

Lord, grant me the grace today to _____

_____

_____

_____

_____

3. Review the Day: Review the day you just lived like a film in your head, paying close attention to moments you felt close to God, those in which you did not, and how you chose to respond in these moments. Then talk to the Lord; share your heart.

Lord, I felt close to you today when _____

_____

_____

_____

_____

4. Ask for Forgiveness: Admit any mistakes you made today and ask God to heal your heart.

Today, Lord, I ask forgiveness for _____

_____

_____

_____

_____

5. Look Forward: Take the insights God has given you today and ask him where he is leading you. What does he want from you tomorrow? Together, in relationship with him and through his grace, prepare yourself to take on the next day.

Today I experienced _____

_____

_____

_____

Tomorrow I am going to focus on _____

_____

_____

_____

_____

☐ *I Lived Day 7 as an Activated Disciple!*

DAY 8

ACTIVATING FORGIVENESS

☐ Watch video: Forgiveness, Part 2

A Word with God – *Lectio Divina*

LECTIO
(READ)

Read **Matthew 5:21-26** slowly, then read it again. Read it a third time. Look for details. Notice key words, verbs and nouns, and anything repeated, compared, or contrasted.

MEDITATIO
(MEDITATE)

Mentally "chew" on the passage's key words or images to extract their meaning. Let the words sink in and take hold. What words or phrases catch and hold your attention?

_____

_____

_____

_____

_____

_____

_____

_____

ORATIO
(PRAY)

Pay attention to the way your meditation connects with your life, and respond to what you find. This is your time to "have a word" with God through his Word! Speak to him in your words. Make it personal. Share your heart: He is listening.

CONTEMPLATIO
(CONTEMPLATE)

Savor being in God's presence. Enjoy what God has given you.

IMITATIO
(IMITATE)

Resolve to act on what God has revealed to you in *lectio divina*. Recall the characteristics of a disciple at the focus of today's Scripture verses. What specific attitude or action of a disciple will you imitate?

_____

_____

_____

_____

_____

_____

A WORD OF ENCOURAGEMENT

"As you get ready to live another day for God, incorporate into your morning prayer a brief review of your relationships and ask the Lord to reveal if you have anything against others. If so, make it a point to rectify that relationship today."

— *Jeff Cavins*

Situational Awareness

Note circumstances during your day that gave you the opportunity to exercise the characteristic of a disciple that God revealed to you in your time with him.

_____

_____

_____

_____

_____

_____

_____

_____

_____

_____

Check-In

Cultivate your ongoing relationship with your saintly posse daily, and work with your accountability partner once a week to discuss your walk with Christ.

☐ Today I checked in with my posse.

☐ Today I checked in with my accountability partner.

The Shape of My Day

1. Express Gratitude: Give thanks to God for the gifts he has given you today.

Today I give thanks for _____

_____

_____

_____

2. Seek Grace: Ask God for the insight to see what he's been trying to reveal to you throughout the day, and for guidance in recognizing the hurdles you faced in trying to do his will.

Lord, grant me the grace today to _____

_____

_____

_____

_____

3. Review the Day: Review the day you just lived like a film in your head, paying close attention to moments you felt close to God, those in which you did not, and how you chose to respond in these moments. Then talk to the Lord; share your heart.

Lord, I felt close to you today when _____

_____

_____

_____

_____

4. Ask for Forgiveness: Admit any mistakes you made today and ask God to heal your heart.

Today, Lord, I ask forgiveness for _____

_____

_____

_____

_____

5. Look Forward: Take the insights God has given you today and ask him where he is leading you. What does he want from you tomorrow? Together, in relationship with him and through his grace, prepare yourself to take on the next day.

Today I experienced _____

_____

_____

_____

_____

Tomorrow I am going to focus on _____

_____

_____

_____

_____

☐ *I Lived Day 8 as an Activated Disciple!*

DAY 9
ACTIVATING FORGIVENESS

A Word with God – *Lectio Divina*

LECTIO
(READ)

Read **Matthew 18:21-35** slowly, then read it again. Read it a third time. Look for details. Notice key words, verbs and nouns, and anything repeated, compared, or contrasted.

MEDITATIO
(MEDITATE)

Mentally "chew" on the passage's key words or images to extract their meaning. Let the words sink in and take hold. What words or phrases catch and hold your attention?

_____

_____

_____

_____

_____

_____

_____

_____

ORATIO
(PRAY)

Pay attention to the way your meditation connects with your life, and respond to what you find. This is your time to "have a word" with God through his Word! Speak to him in your words. Make it personal. Share your heart: He is listening.

CONTEMPLATIO
(CONTEMPLATE)

Savor being in God's presence. Enjoy what God has given you.

IMITATIO
(IMITATE)

Resolve to act on what God has revealed to you in *lectio divina.* Recall the characteristics of a disciple at the focus of today's Scripture verses. What specific attitude or action of a disciple will you imitate?

_____

_____

_____

_____

_____

_____

A WORD OF ENCOURAGEMENT

"It is a very sobering thought to realize that there is a relationship between what we have been forgiven for by the Lord and our willingness to forgive those who have sinned against us. Don't block God's forgiveness from changing you by refusing to forgive others."

— *Jeff Cavins*

Situational Awareness

Note circumstances during your day that gave you the opportunity to exercise the characteristic of a disciple that God revealed to you in your time with him.

_____

_____

_____

_____

_____

_____

_____

_____

_____

_____

Check-In

Cultivate your ongoing relationship with your saintly posse daily, and work with your accountability partner once a week to discuss your walk with Christ.

☐ Today I checked in with my posse.

☐ Today I checked in with my accountability partner.

The Shape of My Day

1. **Express Gratitude:** Give thanks to God for the gifts he has given you today.

   Today I give thanks for _____

   _____

   _____

   _____

2. **Seek Grace:** Ask God for the insight to see what he's been trying to reveal to you throughout the day, and for guidance in recognizing the hurdles you faced in trying to do his will.

   Lord, grant me the grace today to _____

   _____

   _____

   _____

   _____

3. **Review the Day:** Review the day you just lived like a film in your head, paying close attention to moments you felt close to God, those in which you did not, and how you chose to respond in these moments. Then talk to the Lord; share your heart.

   Lord, I felt close to you today when _____

   _____

   _____

   _____

   _____

4. Ask for Forgiveness: Admit any mistakes you made today and ask God to heal your heart.

Today, Lord, I ask forgiveness for _____

_____

_____

_____

5. Look Forward: Take the insights God has given you today and ask him where he is leading you. What does he want from you tomorrow? Together, in relationship with him and through his grace, prepare yourself to take on the next day.

Today I experienced _____

_____

_____

_____

Tomorrow I am going to focus on _____

_____

_____

_____

☐ *I Lived Day 9 as an Activated Disciple!*

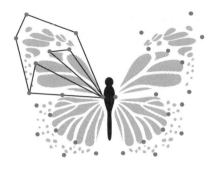

DAY 10
ACTIVATING
FORGIVENESS

A Word with God – *Lectio Divina*

LECTIO
(READ)

Read **John 8:3-11** slowly, then read it again. Read it a third time. Look for details. Notice key words, verbs and nouns, and anything repeated, compared, or contrasted.

MEDITATIO
(MEDITATE)

Mentally "chew" on the passage's key words or images to extract their meaning. Let the words sink in and take hold. What words or phrases catch and hold your attention?

_____

_____

_____

_____

_____

_____

_____

ORATIO
(PRAY)

Pay attention to the way your meditation connects with your life, and respond to what you find. This is your time to "have a word" with God through his Word! Speak to him in your words. Make it personal. Share your heart: He is listening.

CONTEMPLATIO
(CONTEMPLATE)

Savor being in God's presence. Enjoy what God has given you.

IMITATIO
(IMITATE)

Resolve to act on what God has revealed to you in *lectio divina*. Recall the characteristics of a disciple at the focus of today's Scripture verses. What specific attitude or action of a disciple will you imitate?

_____

_____

_____

_____

_____

_____

A WORD OF ENCOURAGEMENT

"Sometimes we tend to delight when others get what is coming to them. Today, I invite you to look through the lens of Christ and pray for God's mercy and forgiveness for those who have done wrong and are broken."

— *Jeff Cavins*

Situational Awareness

Note circumstances during your day that gave you the opportunity to exercise the characteristic of a disciple that God revealed to you in your time with him.

_____

_____

_____

_____

_____

_____

_____

_____

_____

_____

Check-In

Cultivate your ongoing relationship with your saintly posse daily, and work with your accountability partner once a week to discuss your walk with Christ.

☐ Today I checked in with my posse.

☐ Today I checked in with my accountability partner.

The Shape of My Day

1. **Express Gratitude:** Give thanks to God for the gifts he has given you today.

   Today I give thanks for _____

   _____

   _____

   _____

2. **Seek Grace:** Ask God for the insight to see what he's been trying to reveal to you throughout the day, and for guidance in recognizing the hurdles you faced in trying to do his will.

   Lord, grant me the grace today to _____

   _____

   _____

   _____

3. **Review the Day:** Review the day you just lived like a film in your head, paying close attention to moments you felt close to God, those in which you did not, and how you chose to respond in these moments. Then talk to the Lord; share your heart.

   Lord, I felt close to you today when _____

   _____

   _____

   _____

   _____

4. Ask for Forgiveness: Admit any mistakes you made today and ask God to heal your heart.

Today, Lord, I ask forgiveness for _____

_____

_____

_____

_____

5. Look Forward: Take the insights God has given you today and ask him where he is leading you. What does he want from you tomorrow? Together, in relationship with him and through his grace, prepare yourself to take on the next day.

Today I experienced _____

_____

_____

_____

_____

Tomorrow I am going to focus on _____

_____

_____

_____

_____

☐ *I Lived Day 10 as an Activated Disciple!*

NOTES

"The soul's true greatness is in loving God and in humbling oneself in His presence, completely forgetting oneself and believing oneself to be nothing, because the Lord is great, but He is well pleased only with the humble; He always opposes the proud."

— *The Blessed Virgin Mary to St. Faustina*
(Diary, 1711)

HUMILITY

Is there one ingredient to add to your day as an activated disciple that will give you the best chance to get along with people, acquire godly wisdom, and avoid heartache? Yes, and that critical ingredient is humility.

Humility is having a proper assessment of who you are in relation to God and to other people. A proper and healthy relationship with God and others puts you in a place where you can learn, appreciate others, and avoid unnecessary conflict. Walking with a proper understanding of who we are is not something that we casually acknowledge, but rather a purposeful decision that we make every day.

We must avoid a "practical atheism," a phrase coined by St. John Paul II, where we believe in God but live as though he does not exist. When we believe in God but live as though he does not exist, we have a tendency to direct our own lives and make decisions based on our personal interests.

As activated disciples, we must daily turn control of our lives over to Jesus and ask for his guidance, insight, and correction. If we do not make a conscious decision to allow Jesus to "take the wheel," we will become the automatic pilots of our lives and lose sight of his master plan. Life is too busy to live at the speed of tyranny—we must slow down and daily say, "Lord, your will be done in my life."

When you said yes to becoming a disciple of the Lord, you said yes to taking on his yoke. This means that his worldview, his purposes, and his mannerisms are now your goal in life. Humility is the only way you can see these important aspects and the only way you will walk in them.

> Come now, you who say, "Today or tomorrow we will go into such and such a town and spend a year there and trade and get gain"; whereas you do not know about tomorrow. What is your life? For you are a mist that appears for a little time and then vanishes. Instead you ought to say, "If the Lord wills, we shall live and we shall do this or that." (James 4:13-15)

Throughout the day, you will encounter many people. As you spend time with family, coworkers, and new acquaintances, carefully listen to them with a humble heart. Ask the Lord to give you a heart that is open to learning new things instead of insisting on your own way.

Pride is dangerous, as it is the opposite of humility. Pride insists on its own way and puts up walls around your heart and mind, not allowing anything to penetrate or impart wisdom.

At the beginning of every day, the disciple of Christ must undergo a reality check and compare his or her life to Jesus. "And being found in human form he humbled himself and became obedient unto death, even death on a cross" (Philippians 2:8). Obedience is the mark of a humble heart and a defining aspect of an activated disciple.

TALMIDIM CHALLENGE

- Make sure that during your time of *lectio divina*, you consciously focus on what Jesus is saying to you for that day and place his will above your own plans and aspirations.

- Resist boasting about yourself or talking about yourself when others are sharing. "Be quick to hear, slow to speak" (James 1:19).

- In John 13:12-15, Jesus washes the disciples' feet. How can you "wash the feet" of others today at home? At work? With extended family?

DAY 11
ACTIVATING HUMILITY

☐ Watch video: Humility, Part 1

A Word with God – *Lectio Divina*

LECTIO
(READ)

Read **Ephesians 4:1-3** slowly, then read it again. Read it a third time. Look for details. Notice key words, verbs and nouns, and anything repeated, compared, or contrasted.

MEDITATIO
(MEDITATE)

Mentally "chew" on the passage's key words or images to extract their meaning. Let the words sink in and take hold. What words or phrases catch and hold your attention?

_____

_____

_____

_____

_____

_____

_____

ORATIO
(PRAY)

Pay attention to the way your meditation connects with your life, and respond to what you find. This is your time to "have a word" with God through his Word! Speak to him in your words. Make it personal. Share your heart: He is listening.

CONTEMPLATIO
(CONTEMPLATE)

Savor being in God's presence. Enjoy what God has given you.

IMITATIO
(IMITATE)

Resolve to act on what God has revealed to you in *lectio divina*. Recall the characteristics of a disciple at the focus of today's Scripture verses. What specific attitude or action of a disciple will you imitate?

_____

_____

_____

_____

_____

_____

A WORD OF ENCOURAGEMENT

"Quite often when we feel trapped or imprisoned by life's circumstances we can act out in unbecoming ways. Today, respond to those frustrating situations by walking in humility, forbearing one another."

— *Jeff Cavins*

Situational Awareness

Note circumstances during your day that gave you the opportunity to exercise the characteristic of a disciple that God revealed to you in your time with him.

_____

_____

_____

_____

_____

_____

_____

_____

_____

_____

Check-In

Cultivate your ongoing relationship with your saintly posse daily, and work with your accountability partner once a week to discuss your walk with Christ.

☐ Today I checked in with my posse.

☐ Today I checked in with my accountability partner.

The Shape of My Day

1. **Express Gratitude:** Give thanks to God for the gifts he has given you today.

   Today I give thanks for _____

   _____

   _____

   _____

2. **Seek Grace:** Ask God for the insight to see what he's been trying to reveal to you throughout the day, and for guidance in recognizing the hurdles you faced in trying to do his will.

   Lord, grant me the grace today to _____

   _____

   _____

   _____

   _____

3. **Review the Day:** Review the day you just lived like a film in your head, paying close attention to moments you felt close to God, those in which you did not, and how you chose to respond in these moments. Then talk to the Lord; share your heart.

   Lord, I felt close to you today when _____

   _____

   _____

   _____

   _____

4. **Ask for Forgiveness:** Admit any mistakes you made today and ask God to heal your heart.

Today, Lord, I ask forgiveness for _____

_____

_____

_____

_____

5. **Look Forward:** Take the insights God has given you today and ask him where he is leading you. What does he want from you tomorrow? Together, in relationship with him and through his grace, prepare yourself to take on the next day.

Today I experienced _____

_____

_____

_____

_____

Tomorrow I am going to focus on _____

_____

_____

_____

_____

☐ *I Lived Day 11 as an Activated Disciple!*

DAY 12
ACTIVATING
HUMILITY

A Word with God – *Lectio Divina*

LECTIO
(READ)

Read **1 Peter 2:21-25** slowly, then read it again. Read it a third time. Look for details. Notice key words, verbs and nouns, and anything repeated, compared, or contrasted.

MEDITATIO
(MEDITATE)

Mentally "chew" on the passage's key words or images to extract their meaning. Let the words sink in and take hold. What words or phrases catch and hold your attention?

_____

_____

_____

_____

_____

_____

_____

_____

ORATIO
(PRAY)

Pay attention to the way your meditation connects with your life, and respond to what you find. This is your time to "have a word" with God through his Word! Speak to him in your words. Make it personal. Share your heart: He is listening.

CONTEMPLATIO
(CONTEMPLATE)

Savor being in God's presence. Enjoy what God has given you.

IMITATIO
(IMITATE)

Resolve to act on what God has revealed to you in *lectio divina*. Recall the characteristics of a disciple at the focus of today's Scripture verses. What specific attitude or action of a disciple will you imitate?

_____

_____

_____

_____

_____

_____

A WORD OF ENCOURAGEMENT

"Today, when you feel compelled to justify yourself and make sure that everyone knows that you are right or have done nothing wrong, try doing what St. Peter tells us: when reviled or when suffering, entrust yourself to God. This is humility!"

— *Jeff Cavins*

Situational Awareness

Note circumstances during your day that gave you the opportunity to exercise the characteristic of a disciple that God revealed to you in your time with him.

_____

_____

_____

_____

_____

_____

_____

_____

_____

_____

_____

_____

Check-In

Cultivate your ongoing relationship with your saintly posse daily, and work with your accountability partner once a week to discuss your walk with Christ.

☐ Today I checked in with my posse.

☐ Today I checked in with my accountability partner.

The Shape of My Day

1. **Express Gratitude:** Give thanks to God for the gifts he has given you today.

   Today I give thanks for _____

   _____

   _____

   _____

2. **Seek Grace:** Ask God for the insight to see what he's been trying to reveal to you throughout the day, and for guidance in recognizing the hurdles you faced in trying to do his will.

   Lord, grant me the grace today to _____

   _____

   _____

   _____

   _____

3. **Review the Day:** Review the day you just lived like a film in your head, paying close attention to moments you felt close to God, those in which you did not, and how you chose to respond in these moments. Then talk to the Lord; share your heart.

   Lord, I felt close to you today when _____

   _____

   _____

   _____

   _____

4. Ask for Forgiveness: Admit any mistakes you made today and ask God to heal your heart.

Today, Lord, I ask forgiveness for _____

_____

_____

_____

_____

5. Look Forward: Take the insights God has given you today and ask him where he is leading you. What does he want from you tomorrow? Together, in relationship with him and through his grace, prepare yourself to take on the next day.

Today I experienced _____

_____

_____

_____

_____

Tomorrow I am going to focus on _____

_____

_____

_____

_____

☐ *I Lived Day 12 as an Activated Disciple!*

DAY 13
ACTIVATING HUMILITY

☐ Watch video: Humility, Part 2

A Word with God – *Lectio Divina*

LECTIO
(READ)

Read **Proverbs 16:16-21** slowly, then read it again. Read it a third time. Look for details. Notice key words, verbs and nouns, and anything repeated, compared, or contrasted.

MEDITATIO
(MEDITATE)

Mentally "chew" on the passage's key words or images to extract their meaning. Let the words sink in and take hold. What words or phrases catch and hold your attention?

_____

_____

_____

_____

_____

_____

_____

ORATIO
(PRAY)

Pay attention to the way your meditation connects with your life, and respond to what you find. This is your time to "have a word" with God through his Word! Speak to him in your words. Make it personal. Share your heart: He is listening.

CONTEMPLATIO
(CONTEMPLATE)

Savor being in God's presence. Enjoy what God has given you.

IMITATIO
(IMITATE)

Resolve to act on what God has revealed to you in *lectio divina*. Recall the characteristics of a disciple at the focus of today's Scripture verses. What specific attitude or action of a disciple will you imitate?

A WORD OF ENCOURAGEMENT

"The writer of Proverbs contrasts humility with riches. His conclusion
is that you will be better off living with a spirit of humility than
gaining worldly treasures. Today, fill your treasure chest with acts
that proceed from an attitude of humility."

— *Jeff Cavins*

Situational Awareness

Note circumstances during your day that gave you the opportunity to exercise the characteristic of a disciple that God revealed to you in your time with him.

_____

_____

_____

_____

_____

_____

_____

_____

_____

_____

Check-In

Cultivate your ongoing relationship with your saintly posse daily, and work with your accountability partner once a week to discuss your walk with Christ.

☐ Today I checked in with my posse.

☐ Today I checked in with my accountability partner.

The Shape of My Day

1. **Express Gratitude:** Give thanks to God for the gifts he has given you today.

   Today I give thanks for _____

   _____

   _____

   _____

2. **Seek Grace:** Ask God for the insight to see what he's been trying to reveal to you throughout the day, and for guidance in recognizing the hurdles you faced in trying to do his will.

   Lord, grant me the grace today to _____

   _____

   _____

   _____

3. **Review the Day:** Review the day you just lived like a film in your head, paying close attention to moments you felt close to God, those in which you did not, and how you chose to respond in these moments. Then talk to the Lord; share your heart.

   Lord, I felt close to you today when _____

   _____

   _____

   _____

   _____

4. **Ask for Forgiveness:** Admit any mistakes you made today and ask God to heal your heart.

Today, Lord, I ask forgiveness for _____

_____

_____

_____

_____

5. **Look Forward:** Take the insights God has given you today and ask him where he is leading you. What does he want from you tomorrow? Together, in relationship with him and through his grace, prepare yourself to take on the next day.

Today I experienced _____

_____

_____

_____

Tomorrow I am going to focus on _____

_____

_____

_____

☐ *I Lived Day 13 as an Activated Disciple!*

DAY 14
ACTIVATING HUMILITY

A Word with God – *Lectio Divina*

LECTIO
(READ)

Read **Philippians 2:3-8** slowly, then read it again. Read it a third time. Look for details. Notice key words, verbs and nouns, and anything repeated, compared, or contrasted.

MEDITATIO
(MEDITATE)

Mentally "chew" on the passage's key words or images to extract their meaning. Let the words sink in and take hold. What words or phrases catch and hold your attention?

_____

_____

_____

_____

_____

_____

_____

_____

ORATIO
(PRAY)

Pay attention to the way your meditation connects with your life, and respond to what you find. This is your time to "have a word" with God through his Word! Speak to him in your words. Make it personal. Share your heart: He is listening.

CONTEMPLATIO
(CONTEMPLATE)

Savor being in God's presence. Enjoy what God has given you.

IMITATIO
(IMITATE)

Resolve to act on what God has revealed to you in *lectio divina*. Recall the characteristics of a disciple at the focus of today's Scripture verses. What specific attitude or action of a disciple will you imitate?

_____

_____

_____

_____

_____

_____

_____

A WORD OF ENCOURAGEMENT

"Today's reading encourages us to take an interest in others. You can do this by simply asking those you encounter, 'How can I pray for you today?' Often people will bring up situations that are very important to them and will appreciate you praying for them."

— *Jeff Cavins*

Situational Awareness

Note circumstances during your day that gave you the opportunity to exercise the characteristic of a disciple that God revealed to you in your time with him.

_____

_____

_____

_____

_____

_____

_____

_____

_____

_____

Check-In

Cultivate your ongoing relationship with your saintly posse daily, and work with your accountability partner once a week to discuss your walk with Christ.

☐ Today I checked in with my posse.

☐ Today I checked in with my accountability partner.

The Shape of My Day

1. **Express Gratitude:** Give thanks to God for the gifts he has given you today.

   Today I give thanks for _____

   _____

   _____

   _____

2. **Seek Grace:** Ask God for the insight to see what he's been trying to reveal to you throughout the day, and for guidance in recognizing the hurdles you faced in trying to do his will.

   Lord, grant me the grace today to _____

   _____

   _____

   _____

3. **Review the Day:** Review the day you just lived like a film in your head, paying close attention to moments you felt close to God, those in which you did not, and how you chose to respond in these moments. Then talk to the Lord; share your heart.

   Lord, I felt close to you today when _____

   _____

   _____

   _____

   _____

4. Ask for Forgiveness: Admit any mistakes you made today and ask God to heal your heart.

Today, Lord, I ask forgiveness for _____

_____

_____

_____

_____

5. Look Forward: Take the insights God has given you today and ask him where he is leading you. What does he want from you tomorrow? Together, in relationship with him and through his grace, prepare yourself to take on the next day.

Today I experienced _____

_____

_____

_____

Tomorrow I am going to focus on _____

_____

_____

_____

☐ *I Lived Day 14 as an Activated Disciple!*

DAY 15
ACTIVATING HUMILITY

A Word with God – *Lectio Divina*

LECTIO
(READ)

Read **Luke 14:7-11** slowly, then read it again. Read it a third time. Look for details. Notice key words, verbs and nouns, and anything repeated, compared, or contrasted.

MEDITATIO
(MEDITATE)

Mentally "chew" on the passage's key words or images to extract their meaning. Let the words sink in and take hold. What words or phrases catch and hold your attention?

_____

_____

_____

_____

_____

_____

_____

ORATIO
(PRAY)

Pay attention to the way your meditation connects with your life, and respond to what you find. This is your time to "have a word" with God through his Word! Speak to him in your words. Make it personal. Share your heart: He is listening.

CONTEMPLATIO
(CONTEMPLATE)

Savor being in God's presence. Enjoy what God has given you.

IMITATIO
(IMITATE)

Resolve to act on what God has revealed to you in *lectio divina.* Recall the characteristics of a disciple at the focus of today's Scripture verses. What specific attitude or action of a disciple will you imitate?

A WORD OF ENCOURAGEMENT

"We all do it. We like to sit in places of honor and to be recognized for the things we have done. What if you didn't insist on recognition? What if you didn't strive to sit in the place of honor? Ask yourself, 'What would Jesus do?' Then do it!"

— Jeff Cavins

Situational Awareness

Note circumstances during your day that gave you the opportunity to exercise the characteristic of a disciple that God revealed to you in your time with him.

_____

_____

_____

_____

_____

_____

_____

_____

_____

_____

Check-In

Cultivate your ongoing relationship with your saintly posse daily, and work with your accountability partner once a week to discuss your walk with Christ.

☐ Today I checked in with my posse.

☐ Today I checked in with my accountability partner.

The Shape of My Day

1. Express Gratitude: Give thanks to God for the gifts he has given you today.

Today I give thanks for _____

_____

_____

_____

2. Seek Grace: Ask God for the insight to see what he's been trying to reveal to you throughout the day, and for guidance in recognizing the hurdles you faced in trying to do his will.

Lord, grant me the grace today to _____

_____

_____

_____

3. Review the Day: Review the day you just lived like a film in your head, paying close attention to moments you felt close to God, those in which you did not, and how you chose to respond in these moments. Then talk to the Lord; share your heart.

Lord, I felt close to you today when _____

_____

_____

_____

4. Ask for Forgiveness: Admit any mistakes you made today and ask God to heal your heart.

Today, Lord, I ask forgiveness for _____

_____

_____

_____

_____

5. Look Forward: Take the insights God has given you today and ask him where he is leading you. What does he want from you tomorrow? Together, in relationship with him and through his grace, prepare yourself to take on the next day.

Today I experienced _____

_____

_____

_____

_____

Tomorrow I am going to focus on _____

_____

_____

_____

_____

☐ *I Lived Day 15 as an Activated Disciple!*

" The more perfect our patience is,
the more perfectly do we
possess our souls. *"*

— *St. Francis de Sales*

PATIENCE

What would life be like if God were not patient with you? Scary thought, right?

Everyone you meet is somewhere on the continuum of life. Have you ever met anyone who is perfect? Probably not. Patience is about meeting people who are in the process of becoming mature, and adapting yourself to them, but it also extends beyond our relationships to life in general.

Patience is a powerful virtue whereby we strive to be patient in all things for the love of God and neighbor. Impatience is actually a weakness that takes us off the road to holiness. Our love of God and neighbor are compromised when we succumb to impatience. Patience is a virtue that is closely attached to fortitude, which keeps us on track and helps us avoid despair, grumbling, and complaining.

As a disciple of Christ, it is important for you to remember that patience is a virtue; consequently, it is something we need to practice over and over until it becomes a part of us. You can grow in patience, which will give you a much better chance of understanding the heart and plan of Jesus. The disciple knows that ultimately God is in control, and God has his own timetable that must be considered. Providence is a friend of patience, as it always gives room for God's plans to be fulfilled in his time. When we insist on our own timetable, we can become impatient and actually spoil the work that God is trying to do. This is particularly true in our relationships with family, friends, and colleagues.

Our impatience actually provides a false witness, for God is love (1 John 4:8) and love is patient (1 Corinthians 13:4). Today you

will have the opportunity to walk in patience and demonstrate an aspect of love that people desperately need.

An important aspect of patience to keep in mind is that patience is not merely maintaining a passive state of being, a point that is often misunderstood. Patience is not just waiting things out hoping something happens. No, patience waits and at the same time creatively and prayerfully pursues the goal, which is the love of God and neighbor.

Patience without love is an exercise in frustration, but patience motivated by love is productive; it is an opportunity to experience the patience of God in your own life. St. Paul points this out in his letter to the Ephesians, when he asks them to walk "with all lowliness and meekness, with patience, forbearing one another in love, eager to maintain the unity of the Spirit in the bond of peace" (Ephesians 4:2-3).

During your times of frustration, turn to the Lord and make him your focus. Isaiah said, "But they who wait for the LORD shall renew their strength, they shall mount up with wings like eagles, they shall run and not be weary, they shall walk and not faint" (Isaiah 40:31).

TALMIDIM CHALLENGE

- Ask yourself today with whom, where, and when do you need patience? Before encountering these opportunities, pray that you may exercise patience, providence, and fortitude in a way that will lead to the love of God.

- Acknowledge when others, including God, are patient with you, and let them know how appreciative you are.

- If you find that you have become impatient, stop yourself in the midst of it and make the correction that is needed. Take a moment to apologize, and call on the Lord for strength and focus to become more patient.

DAY 16
ACTIVATING PATIENCE

☐ Watch video: Patience, Part 1

A Word with God – *Lectio Divina*

LECTIO
(READ)

Read **James 1:2-4 and 1:12** slowly, then read it again. Read it a third time. Look for details. Notice key words, verbs and nouns, and anything repeated, compared, or contrasted.

MEDITATIO
(MEDITATE)

Mentally "chew" on the passage's key words or images to extract their meaning. Let the words sink in and take hold. What words or phrases catch and hold your attention?

_____

_____

_____

_____

_____

_____

_____

ORATIO
(PRAY)

Pay attention to the way your meditation connects with your life, and respond to what you find. This is your time to "have a word" with God through his Word! Speak to him in your words. Make it personal. Share your heart: He is listening.

CONTEMPLATIO
(CONTEMPLATE)

Savor being in God's presence. Enjoy what God has given you.

IMITATIO
(IMITATE)

Resolve to act on what God has revealed to you in *lectio divina.* Recall the characteristics of a disciple at the focus of today's Scripture verses. What specific attitude or action of a disciple will you imitate?

_____

_____

_____

_____

_____

_____

A WORD OF ENCOURAGEMENT

"Feel like your faith has been tested lately? James tells us that steadfastness is the outcome of trials if we continue in faithfulness. Trials can cause us to want to give up—but don't. The reward of steadfastness is that you will be perfect, complete, and lacking nothing. Not a bad deal!"

— *Jeff Cavins*

Situational Awareness

Note circumstances during your day that gave you the opportunity to exercise the characteristic of a disciple that God revealed to you in your time with him.

_____

_____

_____

_____

_____

_____

_____

_____

_____

_____

Check-In

Cultivate your ongoing relationship with your saintly posse daily, and work with your accountability partner once a week to discuss your walk with Christ.

☐ Today I checked in with my posse.

☐ Today I checked in with my accountability partner.

The Shape of My Day

1. Express Gratitude: Give thanks to God for the gifts he has given you today.

Today I give thanks for _____

_____

_____

_____

2. Seek Grace: Ask God for the insight to see what he's been trying to reveal to you throughout the day, and for guidance in recognizing the hurdles you faced in trying to do his will.

Lord, grant me the grace today to _____

_____

_____

_____

_____

3. Review the Day: Review the day you just lived like a film in your head, paying close attention to moments you felt close to God, those in which you did not, and how you chose to respond in these moments. Then talk to the Lord; share your heart.

Lord, I felt close to you today when _____

_____

_____

_____

_____

4. Ask for Forgiveness: Admit any mistakes you made today and ask God to heal your heart.

Today, Lord, I ask forgiveness for _____

_____

_____

_____

_____

5. Look Forward: Take the insights God has given you today and ask him where he is leading you. What does he want from you tomorrow? Together, in relationship with him and through his grace, prepare yourself to take on the next day.

Today I experienced _____

_____

_____

_____

Tomorrow I am going to focus on _____

_____

_____

_____

☐ *I Lived Day 16 as an Activated Disciple!*

DAY 17
ACTIVATING
PATIENCE

A Word with God – *Lectio Divina*

LECTIO
(READ)

Read **Colossians 3:12-15** slowly, then read it again. Read it a third time. Look for details. Notice key words, verbs and nouns, and anything repeated, compared, or contrasted.

MEDITATIO
(MEDITATE)

Mentally "chew" on the passage's key words or images to extract their meaning. Let the words sink in and take hold. What words or phrases catch and hold your attention?

_____

_____

_____

_____

_____

_____

_____

_____

ORATIO
(PRAY)

Pay attention to the way your meditation connects with your life, and respond to what you find. This is your time to "have a word" with God through his Word! Speak to him in your words. Make it personal. Share your heart: He is listening.

CONTEMPLATIO
(CONTEMPLATE)

Savor being in God's presence. Enjoy what God has given you.

IMITATIO
(IMITATE)

Resolve to act on what God has revealed to you in *lectio divina*. Recall the characteristics of a disciple at the focus of today's Scripture verses. What specific attitude or action of a disciple will you imitate?

_____

_____

_____

_____

_____

_____

A WORD OF ENCOURAGEMENT

"I like that Paul tells the Colossians to 'put on patience.'
One thing that really helps me in the area of patience is something
I do frequently. Before a meeting or an appointment that I know
could be rough, I mentally put on patience, like a garment!"

— *Jeff Cavins*

Situational Awareness

Note circumstances during your day that gave you the opportunity to exercise the characteristic of a disciple that God revealed to you in your time with him.

_____

_____

_____

_____

_____

_____

_____

_____

_____

_____

_____

Check-In

Cultivate your ongoing relationship with your saintly posse daily, and work with your accountability partner once a week to discuss your walk with Christ.

☐ Today I checked in with my posse.

☐ Today I checked in with my accountability partner.

The Shape of My Day

1. Express Gratitude: Give thanks to God for the gifts he has given you today.

Today I give thanks for _____

_____

_____

_____

2. Seek Grace: Ask God for the insight to see what he's been trying to reveal to you throughout the day, and for guidance in recognizing the hurdles you faced in trying to do his will.

Lord, grant me the grace today to _____

_____

_____

_____

3. Review the Day: Review the day you just lived like a film in your head, paying close attention to moments you felt close to God, those in which you did not, and how you chose to respond in these moments. Then talk to the Lord; share your heart.

Lord, I felt close to you today when _____

_____

_____

_____

4. Ask for Forgiveness: Admit any mistakes you made today and ask God to heal your heart.

Today, Lord, I ask forgiveness for _____

_____

_____

_____

_____

5. Look Forward: Take the insights God has given you today and ask him where he is leading you. What does he want from you tomorrow? Together, in relationship with him and through his grace, prepare yourself to take on the next day.

Today I experienced _____

_____

_____

_____

_____

Tomorrow I am going to focus on _____

_____

_____

_____

☐ *I Lived Day 17 as an Activated Disciple!*

DAY 18

ACTIVATING PATIENCE

☐ Watch video: Patience, Part 2

A Word with God – *Lectio Divina*

LECTIO
(READ)

Read **Psalm 86:1-8** slowly, then read it again. Read it a third time. Look for details. Notice key words, verbs and nouns, and anything repeated, compared, or contrasted.

MEDITATIO
(MEDITATE)

Mentally "chew" on the passage's key words or images to extract their meaning. Let the words sink in and take hold. What words or phrases catch and hold your attention?

_____

_____

_____

_____

_____

_____

_____

ORATIO
(PRAY)

Pay attention to the way your meditation connects with your life, and respond to what you find. This is your time to "have a word" with God through his Word! Speak to him in your words. Make it personal. Share your heart: He is listening.

CONTEMPLATIO
(CONTEMPLATE)

Savor being in God's presence. Enjoy what God has given you.

IMITATIO
(IMITATE)

Resolve to act on what God has revealed to you in *lectio divina*. Recall the characteristics of a disciple at the focus of today's Scripture verses. What specific attitude or action of a disciple will you imitate?

_____

_____

_____

_____

_____

_____

A WORD OF ENCOURAGEMENT

"Can you think of one area of your life where you continually fall short when it comes to patience? Today is the day that you can isolate that recurring situation and master it. Ask the Lord to help you in that area and repeatedly reinforce it in quiet prayer: 'Lord, Your will be done.'"

— *Jeff Cavins*

Situational Awareness

Note circumstances during your day that gave you the opportunity to exercise the characteristic of a disciple that God revealed to you in your time with him.

_____

_____

_____

_____

_____

_____

_____

_____

_____

_____

Check-In

Cultivate your ongoing relationship with your saintly posse daily, and work with your accountability partner once a week to discuss your walk with Christ.

☐ Today I checked in with my posse.

☐ Today I checked in with my accountability partner.

The Shape of My Day

1. Express Gratitude: Give thanks to God for the gifts he has given you today.

Today I give thanks for _____

_____

_____

_____

2. Seek Grace: Ask God for the insight to see what he's been trying to reveal to you throughout the day, and for guidance in recognizing the hurdles you faced in trying to do his will.

Lord, grant me the grace today to _____

_____

_____

_____

3. Review the Day: Review the day you just lived like a film in your head, paying close attention to moments you felt close to God, those in which you did not, and how you chose to respond in these moments. Then talk to the Lord; share your heart.

Lord, I felt close to you today when _____

_____

_____

_____

_____

4. Ask for Forgiveness: Admit any mistakes you made today and ask God to heal your heart.

Today, Lord, I ask forgiveness for _____

_____

_____

_____

_____

5. Look Forward: Take the insights God has given you today and ask him where he is leading you. What does he want from you tomorrow? Together, in relationship with him and through his grace, prepare yourself to take on the next day.

Today I experienced _____

_____

_____

_____

_____

Tomorrow I am going to focus on _____

_____

_____

_____

_____

☐ *I Lived Day 18 as an Activated Disciple!*

DAY 19
ACTIVATING PATIENCE

A Word with God – *Lectio Divina*

LECTIO
(READ)

Read **2 Corinthians 6:3-10** slowly, then read it again. Read it a third time. Look for details. Notice key words, verbs and nouns, and anything repeated, compared, or contrasted.

MEDITATIO
(MEDITATE)

Mentally "chew" on the passage's key words or images to extract their meaning. Let the words sink in and take hold. What words or phrases catch and hold your attention?

_____

_____

_____

_____

_____

_____

_____

ORATIO
(PRAY)

Pay attention to the way your meditation connects with your life, and respond to what you find. This is your time to "have a word" with God through his Word! Speak to him in your words. Make it personal. Share your heart: He is listening.

CONTEMPLATIO
(CONTEMPLATE)

Savor being in God's presence. Enjoy what God has given you.

IMITATIO
(IMITATE)

Resolve to act on what God has revealed to you in *lectio divina*. Recall the characteristics of a disciple at the focus of today's Scripture verses. What specific attitude or action of a disciple will you imitate?

_____

_____

_____

_____

_____

_____

A WORD OF ENCOURAGEMENT

"God has a calling on your life today. You are called to change the world through your words and actions. Entrust yourself to God through the difficulties of your day and out of it will come a beautiful witness rather than a laundry list of problems."

— *Jeff Cavins*

Situational Awareness

Note circumstances during your day that gave you the opportunity to exercise the characteristic of a disciple that God revealed to you in your time with him.

_____

_____

_____

_____

_____

_____

_____

_____

_____

Check-In

Cultivate your ongoing relationship with your saintly posse daily, and work with your accountability partner once a week to discuss your walk with Christ.

☐ Today I checked in with my posse.

☐ Today I checked in with my accountability partner.

The Shape of My Day

1. Express Gratitude: Give thanks to God for the gifts he has given you today.

Today I give thanks for _____

_____

_____

_____

2. Seek Grace: Ask God for the insight to see what he's been trying to reveal to you throughout the day, and for guidance in recognizing the hurdles you faced in trying to do his will.

Lord, grant me the grace today to _____

_____

_____

_____

_____

3. Review the Day: Review the day you just lived like a film in your head, paying close attention to moments you felt close to God, those in which you did not, and how you chose to respond in these moments. Then talk to the Lord; share your heart.

Lord, I felt close to you today when _____

_____

_____

_____

_____

4. Ask for Forgiveness: Admit any mistakes you made today and ask God to heal your heart.

Today, Lord, I ask forgiveness for _____

_____

_____

_____

_____

5. Look Forward: Take the insights God has given you today and ask him where he is leading you. What does he want from you tomorrow? Together, in relationship with him and through his grace, prepare yourself to take on the next day.

Today I experienced _____

_____

_____

_____

_____

Tomorrow I am going to focus on _____

_____

_____

_____

_____

☐ *I Lived Day 19 as an Activated Disciple!*

DAY 20
ACTIVATING PATIENCE

A Word with God – *Lectio Divina*

LECTIO
(READ)

Read **James 1:1-6** slowly, then read it again. Read it a third time. Look for details. Notice key words, verbs and nouns, and anything repeated, compared, or contrasted.

MEDITATIO
(MEDITATE)

Mentally "chew" on the passage's key words or images to extract their meaning. Let the words sink in and take hold. What words or phrases catch and hold your attention?

_____

_____

_____

_____

_____

_____

_____

_____

ORATIO
(PRAY)

Pay attention to the way your meditation connects with your life, and respond to what you find. This is your time to "have a word" with God through his Word! Speak to him in your words. Make it personal. Share your heart: He is listening.

CONTEMPLATIO
(CONTEMPLATE)

Savor being in God's presence. Enjoy what God has given you.

IMITATIO
(IMITATE)

Resolve to act on what God has revealed to you in *lectio divina*. Recall the characteristics of a disciple at the focus of today's Scripture verses. What specific attitude or action of a disciple will you imitate?

_____

_____

_____

_____

_____

_____

A WORD OF ENCOURAGEMENT

"Oftentimes we face trials and difficulties that only end in frustration. Do something today that is simple yet at the same time profound. Go to a place where you can be alone and verbally ask God for wisdom for your situation. Throughout the day, look for the answer."

— *Jeff Cavins*

Situational Awareness

Note circumstances during your day that gave you the opportunity to exercise the characteristic of a disciple that God revealed to you in your time with him.

_____

_____

_____

_____

_____

_____

_____

_____

_____

_____

Check-In

Cultivate your ongoing relationship with your saintly posse daily, and work with your accountability partner once a week to discuss your walk with Christ.

☐ Today I checked in with my posse.

☐ Today I checked in with my accountability partner.

The Shape of My Day

1. **Express Gratitude:** Give thanks to God for the gifts he has given you today.

   Today I give thanks for _____

   _____

   _____

   _____

2. **Seek Grace:** Ask God for the insight to see what he's been trying to reveal to you throughout the day, and for guidance in recognizing the hurdles you faced in trying to do his will.

   Lord, grant me the grace today to _____

   _____

   _____

   _____

   _____

3. **Review the Day:** Review the day you just lived like a film in your head, paying close attention to moments you felt close to God, those in which you did not, and how you chose to respond in these moments. Then talk to the Lord; share your heart.

   Lord, I felt close to you today when _____

   _____

   _____

   _____

   _____

4. Ask for Forgiveness: Admit any mistakes you made today and ask God to heal your heart.

Today, Lord, I ask forgiveness for _____

_____

_____

_____

_____

5. Look Forward: Take the insights God has given you today and ask him where he is leading you. What does he want from you tomorrow? Together, in relationship with him and through his grace, prepare yourself to take on the next day.

Today I experienced _____

_____

_____

_____

_____

Tomorrow I am going to focus on _____

_____

_____

_____

_____

☐ *I Lived Day 20 as an Activated Disciple!*

" Lord, make me an instrument of your peace: Where there is hatred, let me sow love; where there is injury, pardon; where there is doubt, faith; where there is despair, hope; where there is darkness, light; and where there is sadness, joy. "

— *St. Francis of Assisi*

SELFLESSNESS

Can you live your life in such a way that you can accomplish the will of the Lord for yourself and at the same time live in a selfless manner? The answer is yes, but only if you are conscious of the fact that the Lord is interested in working not only in you but through you as well.

For the activated disciple, it is critically important to realize that your life is not all about you—it's about God's will. Throughout the day, God is looking for opportunities to reach others and invite them to become his adopted sons and daughters. The only way this is going to happen is if his disciples resist focusing only on their lives and allow the Lord to see, reach out, and touch others. Selflessness is what enables us to live in such a way.

For the disciple, there is a link between your relationship with the Lord and looking out for the interests of others: "And the King will answer them, 'Truly, I say to you, as you did it to one of the least of these my brethren, you did it to me'" (Matthew 25:40).

To have the mind of Christ means that we live in a selfless manner: "Let each of you look not only to his own interests, but also to the interests of others. Have this mind among yourselves, which was in Christ Jesus" (Philippians 2:4-5).

One way that you can demonstrate selflessness is by being sensitive to the weaknesses of the people around you. To have a magnanimous heart is to be generous and forgiving, especially toward a rival or someone less powerful than yourself. Paul wrote to the Romans saying, "We who are strong ought to bear with the failings of the weak, and not to please ourselves; let each of us please his neighbor for his good, to edify him" (Romans 15:1-2).

A sign found on a wall at Shishu Bhavan, St. Teresa of Calcutta's home for children in India, is a good reminder of the importance of doing right and living in a selfless way even though we may not get credit or receive any acknowledgment for it:

People are unreasonable, illogical, and self-centered.
Love them anyway.

If you do good,
people will accuse you of selfish, ulterior motives.
Do good anyway.

If you are successful,
you will win false friends and true enemies.
Succeed anyway.

The good you do will be forgotten tomorrow.
Do good anyway.

Honesty and frankness make you vulnerable.
Be honest and frank anyway.

What you spend years building
may be destroyed overnight.
Build anyway.

People really need help
but may attack you if you help them.
Help people anyway.

Give the world the best you have,
and you'll get kicked in the teeth.
Give the world the best you have anyway.[1]

---

[1] Lucinda Vardey, *Mother Teresa: A Simple Path* (New York: Ballantine Books, 1995), 185. The text is closely based on "The Paradoxical Commandments," by Kent M. Keith.

TALMIDIM CHALLENGE

- Selflessness is having the best day of your life and upon meeting a friend, you ask, "How was your day?" Today, find out about others and how they are doing.

- How can you look to the interests of others today?

- Look for small opportunities throughout the day to act and think selflessly. The moment you get an opportunity, seize it.

DAY 21
ACTIVATING SELFLESSNESS

☐ Watch video: Selflessness, Part 1

A Word with God – *Lectio Divina*

LECTIO
(READ)

Read **John 12:23-26** slowly, then read it again. Read it a third time. Look for details. Notice key words, verbs and nouns, and anything repeated, compared, or contrasted.

MEDITATIO
(MEDITATE)

Mentally "chew" on the passage's key words or images to extract their meaning. Let the words sink in and take hold. What words or phrases catch and hold your attention?

_____

_____

_____

_____

_____

_____

_____

ORATIO
(PRAY)

Pay attention to the way your meditation connects with your life, and respond to what you find. This is your time to "have a word" with God through his Word! Speak to him in your words. Make it personal. Share your heart: He is listening.

CONTEMPLATIO
(CONTEMPLATE)

Savor being in God's presence. Enjoy what God has given you.

IMITATIO
(IMITATE)

Resolve to act on what God has revealed to you in *lectio divina*. Recall the characteristics of a disciple at the focus of today's Scripture verses. What specific attitude or action of a disciple will you imitate?

_____

_____

_____

_____

_____

_____

_____

A WORD OF ENCOURAGEMENT

"I have found that the secret to finding my life was losing it in service to Christ. It doesn't make sense to the world, but it works. We more clearly understand who we are and what our purpose in life is when we empty ourselves in God's mission."

— *Jeff Cavins*

Situational Awareness

Note circumstances during your day that gave you the opportunity to exercise the characteristic of a disciple that God revealed to you in your time with him.

_____

_____

_____

_____

_____

_____

_____

_____

_____

Check-In

Cultivate your ongoing relationship with your saintly posse daily, and work with your accountability partner once a week to discuss your walk with Christ.

☐ Today I checked in with my posse.

☐ Today I checked in with my accountability partner.

The Shape of My Day

1. Express Gratitude: Give thanks to God for the gifts he has given you today.

Today I give thanks for _____

_____

_____

_____

2. Seek Grace: Ask God for the insight to see what he's been trying to reveal to you throughout the day, and for guidance in recognizing the hurdles you faced in trying to do his will.

Lord, grant me the grace today to _____

_____

_____

_____

3. Review the Day: Review the day you just lived like a film in your head, paying close attention to moments you felt close to God, those in which you did not, and how you chose to respond in these moments. Then talk to the Lord; share your heart.

Lord, I felt close to you today when _____

_____

_____

_____

4. Ask for Forgiveness: Admit any mistakes you made today and ask God to heal your heart.

Today, Lord, I ask forgiveness for _____

_____

_____

_____

_____

5. Look Forward: Take the insights God has given you today and ask him where he is leading you. What does he want from you tomorrow? Together, in relationship with him and through his grace, prepare yourself to take on the next day.

Today I experienced _____

_____

_____

_____

_____

Tomorrow I am going to focus on _____

_____

_____

_____

_____

☐ *I Lived Day 21 as an Activated Disciple!*

DAY 22
ACTIVATING
SELFLESSNESS

A Word with God – *Lectio Divina*

LECTIO
(READ)

Read **2 Corinthians 4:8-11** slowly, then read it again. Read it a third time. Look for details. Notice key words, verbs and nouns, and anything repeated, compared, or contrasted.

MEDITATIO
(MEDITATE)

Mentally "chew" on the passage's key words or images to extract their meaning. Let the words sink in and take hold. What words or phrases catch and hold your attention?

_____

_____

_____

_____

_____

_____

_____

ORATIO
(PRAY)

Pay attention to the way your meditation connects with your life, and respond to what you find. This is your time to "have a word" with God through his Word! Speak to him in your words. Make it personal. Share your heart: He is listening.

CONTEMPLATIO
(CONTEMPLATE)

Savor being in God's presence. Enjoy what God has given you.

IMITATIO
(IMITATE)

Resolve to act on what God has revealed to you in *lectio divina*. Recall the characteristics of a disciple at the focus of today's Scripture verses. What specific attitude or action of a disciple will you imitate?

_____

_____

_____

_____

_____

_____

_____

A WORD OF ENCOURAGEMENT

"As Christians, we daily die to ourselves so that the life of Christ will be made manifest. This is the key to letting Jesus shine through you—you must diminish, and he must increase! You can experience this by acting selflessly when facing perplexing situations."

— *Jeff Cavins*

Situational Awareness

Note circumstances during your day that gave you the opportunity to exercise the characteristic of a disciple that God revealed to you in your time with him.

_____

_____

_____

_____

_____

_____

_____

_____

_____

_____

Check-In

Cultivate your ongoing relationship with your saintly posse daily, and work with your accountability partner once a week to discuss your walk with Christ.

☐ Today I checked in with my posse.

☐ Today I checked in with my accountability partner.

The Shape of My Day

1. Express Gratitude: Give thanks to God for the gifts he has given you today.

Today I give thanks for _____

_____

_____

_____

2. Seek Grace: Ask God for the insight to see what he's been trying to reveal to you throughout the day, and for guidance in recognizing the hurdles you faced in trying to do his will.

Lord, grant me the grace today to _____

_____

_____

_____

3. Review the Day: Review the day you just lived like a film in your head, paying close attention to moments you felt close to God, those in which you did not, and how you chose to respond in these moments. Then talk to the Lord; share your heart.

Lord, I felt close to you today when _____

_____

_____

_____

_____

4. Ask for Forgiveness: Admit any mistakes you made today and ask God to heal your heart.

Today, Lord, I ask forgiveness for _____

_____

_____

_____

_____

5. Look Forward: Take the insights God has given you today and ask him where he is leading you. What does he want from you tomorrow? Together, in relationship with him and through his grace, prepare yourself to take on the next day.

Today I experienced _____

_____

_____

_____

_____

Tomorrow I am going to focus on _____

_____

_____

_____

_____

☐ *I Lived Day 22 as an Activated Disciple!*

DAY 23

ACTIVATING
SELFLESSNESS

☐ Watch video: Selflessness, Part 2

A Word with God – *Lectio Divina*

LECTIO
(READ)

Read **Luke 1:46-56** slowly, then read it again. Read it a third time. Look for details. Notice key words, verbs and nouns, and anything repeated, compared, or contrasted.

MEDITATIO
(MEDITATE)

Mentally "chew" on the passage's key words or images to extract their meaning. Let the words sink in and take hold. What words or phrases catch and hold your attention?

_____

_____

_____

_____

_____

_____

_____

ORATIO
(PRAY)

Pay attention to the way your meditation connects with your life, and respond to what you find. This is your time to "have a word" with God through his Word! Speak to him in your words. Make it personal. Share your heart: He is listening.

CONTEMPLATIO
(CONTEMPLATE)

Savor being in God's presence. Enjoy what God has given you.

IMITATIO
(IMITATE)

Resolve to act on what God has revealed to you in *lectio divina*. Recall the characteristics of a disciple at the focus of today's Scripture verses. What specific attitude or action of a disciple will you imitate?

_____

_____

_____

_____

_____

_____

A WORD OF ENCOURAGEMENT

"There is something so beautiful about a selfless person.
I often think about St. Teresa of Calcutta and her unending selflessness. She is beautiful in the way that the Blessed Virgin Mary is beautiful. People regard their low estate."

— *Jeff Cavins*

Situational Awareness

Note circumstances during your day that gave you the opportunity to exercise the characteristic of a disciple that God revealed to you in your time with him.

_____

_____

_____

_____

_____

_____

_____

_____

_____

_____

Check-In

Cultivate your ongoing relationship with your saintly posse daily, and work with your accountability partner once a week to discuss your walk with Christ.

☐ Today I checked in with my posse.

☐ Today I checked in with my accountability partner.

The Shape of My Day

1. Express Gratitude: Give thanks to God for the gifts he has given you today.

Today I give thanks for _____

_____

_____

_____

2. Seek Grace: Ask God for the insight to see what he's been trying to reveal to you throughout the day, and for guidance in recognizing the hurdles you faced in trying to do his will.

Lord, grant me the grace today to _____

_____

_____

_____

3. Review the Day: Review the day you just lived like a film in your head, paying close attention to moments you felt close to God, those in which you did not, and how you chose to respond in these moments. Then talk to the Lord; share your heart.

Lord, I felt close to you today when _____

_____

_____

_____

4. Ask for Forgiveness: Admit any mistakes you made today and ask God to heal your heart.

Today, Lord, I ask forgiveness for _____

_____

_____

_____

5. Look Forward: Take the insights God has given you today and ask him where he is leading you. What does he want from you tomorrow? Together, in relationship with him and through his grace, prepare yourself to take on the next day.

Today I experienced _____

_____

_____

_____

Tomorrow I am going to focus on _____

_____

_____

_____

☐ *I Lived Day 23 as an Activated Disciple!*

DAY 24
ACTIVATING SELFLESSNESS

A Word with God – *Lectio Divina*

LECTIO
(READ)

Read **Matthew 9:35-38** slowly, then read it again. Read it a third time. Look for details. Notice key words, verbs and nouns, and anything repeated, compared, or contrasted.

MEDITATIO
(MEDITATE)

Mentally "chew" on the passage's key words or images to extract their meaning. Let the words sink in and take hold. What words or phrases catch and hold your attention?

_____

_____

_____

_____

_____

_____

_____

ORATIO
(PRAY)

Pay attention to the way your meditation connects with your life, and respond to what you find. This is your time to "have a word" with God through his Word! Speak to him in your words. Make it personal. Share your heart: He is listening.

CONTEMPLATIO
(CONTEMPLATE)

Savor being in God's presence. Enjoy what God has given you.

IMITATIO
(IMITATE)

Resolve to act on what God has revealed to you in *lectio divina.* Recall the characteristics of a disciple at the focus of today's Scripture verses. What specific attitude or action of a disciple will you imitate?

_____

_____

_____

_____

_____

_____

A WORD OF ENCOURAGEMENT

"Living with our eyes wide open, we can't help but see the needs around us. Truly, people appear as sheep without a shepherd. Today, participate in the work of the Great Shepherd by speaking words of hope, healing, and compassion."

— *Jeff Cavins*

Situational Awareness

Note circumstances during your day that gave you the opportunity to exercise the characteristic of a disciple that God revealed to you in your time with him.

_____

_____

_____

_____

_____

_____

_____

_____

_____

_____

Check-In

Cultivate your ongoing relationship with your saintly posse daily, and work with your accountability partner once a week to discuss your walk with Christ.

☐ Today I checked in with my posse.

☐ Today I checked in with my accountability partner.

The Shape of My Day

1. **Express Gratitude:** Give thanks to God for the gifts he has given you today.

   Today I give thanks for _____

   _____

   _____

   _____

2. **Seek Grace:** Ask God for the insight to see what he's been trying to reveal to you throughout the day, and for guidance in recognizing the hurdles you faced in trying to do his will.

   Lord, grant me the grace today to _____

   _____

   _____

   _____

3. **Review the Day:** Review the day you just lived like a film in your head, paying close attention to moments you felt close to God, those in which you did not, and how you chose to respond in these moments. Then talk to the Lord; share your heart.

   Lord, I felt close to you today when _____

   _____

   _____

   _____

4. Ask for Forgiveness: Admit any mistakes you made today and ask God to heal your heart.

Today, Lord, I ask forgiveness for _____

_____

_____

_____

5. Look Forward: Take the insights God has given you today and ask him where he is leading you. What does he want from you tomorrow? Together, in relationship with him and through his grace, prepare yourself to take on the next day.

Today I experienced _____

_____

_____

_____

Tomorrow I am going to focus on _____

_____

_____

_____

☐ *I Lived Day 24 as an Activated Disciple!*

DAY 25
ACTIVATING SELFLESSNESS

A Word with God – *Lectio Divina*

LECTIO
(READ)

Read **Luke 6:27-31** slowly, then read it again. Read it a third time. Look for details. Notice key words, verbs and nouns, and anything repeated, compared, or contrasted.

MEDITATIO
(MEDITATE)

Mentally "chew" on the passage's key words or images to extract their meaning. Let the words sink in and take hold. What words or phrases catch and hold your attention?

ORATIO
(PRAY)

Pay attention to the way your meditation connects with your life, and respond to what you find. This is your time to "have a word" with God through his Word! Speak to him in your words. Make it personal. Share your heart: He is listening.

CONTEMPLATIO
(CONTEMPLATE)

Savor being in God's presence. Enjoy what God has given you.

IMITATIO
(IMITATE)

Resolve to act on what God has revealed to you in *lectio divina*. Recall the characteristics of a disciple at the focus of today's Scripture verses. What specific attitude or action of a disciple will you imitate?

_____

_____

_____

_____

_____

_____

A WORD OF ENCOURAGEMENT

"Have you ever experienced what it is like to actually love someone who hates you? I'm reminded of St. John Paul II and how he sat down with and loved the man who shot him. He forgave Mehmet Ali Agca, who later was pardoned at the pope's request. How's your day going?"

— *Jeff Cavins*

Situational Awareness

Note circumstances during your day that gave you the opportunity to exercise the characteristic of a disciple that God revealed to you in your time with him.

_____

_____

_____

_____

_____

_____

_____

_____

_____

_____

Check-In

Cultivate your ongoing relationship with your saintly posse daily, and work with your accountability partner once a week to discuss your walk with Christ.

☐ Today I checked in with my posse.

☐ Today I checked in with my accountability partner.

The Shape of My Day

1. **Express Gratitude:** Give thanks to God for the gifts he has given you today.

   Today I give thanks for _____

   _____

   _____

   _____

2. **Seek Grace:** Ask God for the insight to see what he's been trying to reveal to you throughout the day, and for guidance in recognizing the hurdles you faced in trying to do his will.

   Lord, grant me the grace today to _____

   _____

   _____

   _____

3. **Review the Day:** Review the day you just lived like a film in your head, paying close attention to moments you felt close to God, those in which you did not, and how you chose to respond in these moments. Then talk to the Lord; share your heart.

   Lord, I felt close to you today when _____

   _____

   _____

   _____

4. **Ask for Forgiveness:** Admit any mistakes you made today and ask God to heal your heart.

Today, Lord, I ask forgiveness for _____

_____

_____

_____

_____

5. **Look Forward:** Take the insights God has given you today and ask him where he is leading you. What does he want from you tomorrow? Together, in relationship with him and through his grace, prepare yourself to take on the next day.

Today I experienced _____

_____

_____

_____

_____

Tomorrow I am going to focus on _____

_____

_____

_____

_____

☐ *I Lived Day 25 as an Activated Disciple!*

NOTES

" This shall be my life ... to miss no single opportunity of making some small sacrifice, here by a smiling look, there by a kindly word, always doing the tiniest things right and doing it for love. "

— *St. Thérèse of Lisieux*

KINDNESS

If your busy schedule doesn't permit you to spend long periods of time with the people you meet, is there something you can do to leave them a "spiritual business card"? Yes, be kind. Kindness is a mark of a disciple of Christ.

The saying "Actions speak louder than words" is often true. The kindness we show often surprises people, because they weren't expecting it, and it opened their hearts to God's love.

As you spend time with Jesus in prayer, there will be fruit that comes from your relationship. Kindness is one of the fruits of the Spirit and is a manifestation of life in the Spirit. Kindness is like a gathering of virtues that creates a beautiful bouquet, which touches the hearts of those we meet.

To be kind is to be friendly, generous, and considerate. Usually accompanied by gentleness, patience, and tenderness, kindness has the potential to positively affect others' lives.

When you are kind to others, you have the opportunity to demonstrate the kindness of God. When describing the fall of our first parents, Adam and Eve, the *Catechism of the Catholic Church* points out just how critical kindness is: "The beginning of sin and of man's fall was due to a lie of the tempter who induced doubt of God's word, kindness, and faithfulness" (CCC 215).

You are going to encounter many people who doubt God and his Church. They doubt his Word (Sacred Scripture and Sacred Tradition), his faithfulness, and even his kindness. As a disciple of Jesus, you have been given the task of showing the kindness of God at home, at work, and among your friends.

St. Paul tells us that "in the coming ages he might show the immeasurable riches of his grace in kindness toward us in Christ Jesus" (Ephesians 2:7). As activated disciples, we have the opportunity to imitate God when we are kind to others. Kindness, while not the same as love, certainly leads to the life-changing power of God's love. We are to "be kind to one another, tenderhearted, forgiving one another, as God in Christ forgave you. Therefore, be imitators of God, as beloved children (Ephesians 4:32–5:1).

Kindness is about imitating Christ. It can be given to anyone, anywhere, at any time. Kindness is without prejudice and freely offered. Before today is over, do some intentional acts of kindness. God's kindness wasn't random, and your kindness isn't either.

TALMIDIM CHALLENGE

- If there is someone you know who is struggling, make a point of being kind to them. "Or do you presume upon the riches of his kindness and forbearance and patience? Do you not know that God's kindness is meant to lead you to repentance?" (Romans 2:4).

- In your prayer time, ask God to give you a love for kindness. Pray that he will do work in your heart that will spill over into acts of kindness. "He has showed you, O man, what is good; and what does the Lord require of you but to do justice, and to love kindness, and to walk humbly with your God?" (Micah 6:8).

- God's kindness isn't "random"—it's purposeful. When you see an opportunity to act in kindness, seize it.

DAY 26

ACTIVATING KINDNESS

☐ Watch video: Kindness, Part 1

A Word with God – *Lectio Divina*

LECTIO
(READ)

Read **Ruth 1:14-18** slowly, then read it again. Read it a third time. Look for details. Notice key words, verbs and nouns, and anything repeated, compared, or contrasted.

MEDITATIO
(MEDITATE)

Mentally "chew" on the passage's key words or images to extract their meaning. Let the words sink in and take hold. What words or phrases catch and hold your attention?

_____

_____

_____

_____

_____

_____

_____

_____

ORATIO
(PRAY)

Pay attention to the way your meditation connects with your life, and respond to what you find. This is your time to "have a word" with God through his Word! Speak to him in your words. Make it personal. Share your heart: He is listening.

CONTEMPLATIO
(CONTEMPLATE)

Savor being in God's presence. Enjoy what God has given you.

IMITATIO
(IMITATE)

Resolve to act on what God has revealed to you in *lectio divina.* Recall the characteristics of a disciple at the focus of today's Scripture verses. What specific attitude or action of a disciple will you imitate?

_____

_____

_____

_____

_____

_____

_____

A WORD OF ENCOURAGEMENT

"I have found that when people exhibit unusual kindness, I'm attracted to them and want to become like them. Think about those in your life who could use a little kindness today. Be creative in how you show kindness. Oftentimes people are deeply touched when they didn't expect the kindness."

— *Jeff Cavins*

Situational Awareness

Note circumstances during your day that gave you the opportunity to exercise the characteristic of a disciple that God revealed to you in your time with him.

_____

_____

_____

_____

_____

_____

_____

_____

_____

_____

Check-In

Cultivate your ongoing relationship with your saintly posse daily, and work with your accountability partner once a week to discuss your walk with Christ.

☐ Today I checked in with my posse.

☐ Today I checked in with my accountability partner.

The Shape of My Day

1. Express Gratitude: Give thanks to God for the gifts he has given you today.

Today I give thanks for _____

_____

_____

_____

2. Seek Grace: Ask God for the insight to see what he's been trying to reveal to you throughout the day, and for guidance in recognizing the hurdles you faced in trying to do his will.

Lord, grant me the grace today to _____

_____

_____

_____

3. Review the Day: Review the day you just lived like a film in your head, paying close attention to moments you felt close to God, those in which you did not, and how you chose to respond in these moments. Then talk to the Lord; share your heart.

Lord, I felt close to you today when _____

_____

_____

_____

_____

4. Ask for Forgiveness: Admit any mistakes you made today and ask God to heal your heart.

Today, Lord, I ask forgiveness for _____

_____

_____

_____

_____

5. Look Forward: Take the insights God has given you today and ask him where he is leading you. What does he want from you tomorrow? Together, in relationship with him and through his grace, prepare yourself to take on the next day.

Today I experienced _____

_____

_____

_____

Tomorrow I am going to focus on _____

_____

_____

_____

_____

☐ *I Lived Day 26 as an Activated Disciple!*

DAY 27
ACTIVATING KINDNESS

A Word with God – *Lectio Divina*

LECTIO
(READ)

Read **Titus 3:1-7** slowly, then read it again. Read it a third time. Look for details. Notice key words, verbs and nouns, and anything repeated, compared, or contrasted.

MEDITATIO
(MEDITATE)

Mentally "chew" on the passage's key words or images to extract their meaning. Let the words sink in and take hold. What words or phrases catch and hold your attention?

_____

_____

_____

_____

_____

_____

_____

ORATIO
(PRAY)

Pay attention to the way your meditation connects with your life, and respond to what you find. This is your time to "have a word" with God through his Word! Speak to him in your words. Make it personal. Share your heart: He is listening.

CONTEMPLATIO
(CONTEMPLATE)

Savor being in God's presence. Enjoy what God has given you.

IMITATIO
(IMITATE)

Resolve to act on what God has revealed to you in *lectio divina*. Recall the characteristics of a disciple at the focus of today's Scripture verses. What specific attitude or action of a disciple will you imitate?

_____

_____

_____

_____

_____

_____

_____

A WORD OF ENCOURAGEMENT

"Over the years I have observed that arguments and disagreements result in calm when someone interjects kindness into the situation. Today, be the one who brings kindness to a tumultuous meeting or situation."

— *Jeff Cavins*

Situational Awareness

Note circumstances during your day that gave you the opportunity to exercise the characteristic of a disciple that God revealed to you in your time with him.

_____

_____

_____

_____

_____

_____

_____

_____

_____

_____

_____

Check-In

Cultivate your ongoing relationship with your saintly posse daily, and work with your accountability partner once a week to discuss your walk with Christ.

☐ Today I checked in with my posse.

☐ Today I checked in with my accountability partner.

The Shape of My Day

1. **Express Gratitude:** Give thanks to God for the gifts he has given you today.

   Today I give thanks for _____

   _____

   _____

   _____

2. **Seek Grace:** Ask God for the insight to see what he's been trying to reveal to you throughout the day, and for guidance in recognizing the hurdles you faced in trying to do his will.

   Lord, grant me the grace today to _____

   _____

   _____

   _____

   _____

3. **Review the Day:** Review the day you just lived like a film in your head, paying close attention to moments you felt close to God, those in which you did not, and how you chose to respond in these moments. Then talk to the Lord; share your heart.

   Lord, I felt close to you today when _____

   _____

   _____

   _____

   _____

4. Ask for Forgiveness: Admit any mistakes you made today and ask God to heal your heart.

Today, Lord, I ask forgiveness for _____

_____

_____

_____

_____

5. Look Forward: Take the insights God has given you today and ask him where he is leading you. What does he want from you tomorrow? Together, in relationship with him and through his grace, prepare yourself to take on the next day.

Today I experienced _____

_____

_____

_____

_____

Tomorrow I am going to focus on _____

_____

_____

_____

_____

☐ *I Lived Day 27 as an Activated Disciple!*

DAY 28
ACTIVATING KINDNESS

☐ Watch video: Kindness, Part 2

A Word with God – *Lectio Divina*

LECTIO
(READ)

Read **Luke 5:29-32** slowly, then read it again. Read it a third time. Look for details. Notice key words, verbs and nouns, and anything repeated, compared, or contrasted.

MEDITATIO
(MEDITATE)

Mentally "chew" on the passage's key words or images to extract their meaning. Let the words sink in and take hold. What words or phrases catch and hold your attention?

_____

_____

_____

_____

_____

_____

_____

ORATIO
(PRAY)

Pay attention to the way your meditation connects with your life, and respond to what you find. This is your time to "have a word" with God through his Word! Speak to him in your words. Make it personal. Share your heart: He is listening.

CONTEMPLATIO
(CONTEMPLATE)

Savor being in God's presence. Enjoy what God has given you.

IMITATIO
(IMITATE)

Resolve to act on what God has revealed to you in *lectio divina.* Recall the characteristics of a disciple at the focus of today's Scripture verses. What specific attitude or action of a disciple will you imitate?

_____

_____

_____

_____

_____

_____

A WORD OF ENCOURAGEMENT

"There are certain people in society who most would agree should not be treated with kindness. In Jesus' day it was the tax collectors who were fair game. We must respond to these people differently than the world responds. We respond with kindness."

— *Jeff Cavins*

Situational Awareness

Note circumstances during your day that gave you the opportunity to exercise the characteristic of a disciple that God revealed to you in your time with him.

_____

_____

_____

_____

_____

_____

_____

_____

_____

_____

Check-In

Cultivate your ongoing relationship with your saintly posse daily, and work with your accountability partner once a week to discuss your walk with Christ.

☐ Today I checked in with my posse.

☐ Today I checked in with my accountability partner.

The Shape of My Day

1. Express Gratitude: Give thanks to God for the gifts he has given you today.

Today I give thanks for _____

_____

_____

_____

2. Seek Grace: Ask God for the insight to see what he's been trying to reveal to you throughout the day, and for guidance in recognizing the hurdles you faced in trying to do his will.

Lord, grant me the grace today to _____

_____

_____

_____

3. Review the Day: Review the day you just lived like a film in your head, paying close attention to moments you felt close to God, those in which you did not, and how you chose to respond in these moments. Then talk to the Lord; share your heart.

Lord, I felt close to you today when _____

_____

_____

_____

4. **Ask for Forgiveness:** Admit any mistakes you made today and ask God to heal your heart.

Today, Lord, I ask forgiveness for _____

_____

_____

_____

_____

5. **Look Forward:** Take the insights God has given you today and ask him where he is leading you. What does he want from you tomorrow? Together, in relationship with him and through his grace, prepare yourself to take on the next day.

Today I experienced _____

_____

_____

_____

_____

Tomorrow I am going to focus on _____

_____

_____

_____

_____

☐ *I Lived Day 28 as an Activated Disciple!*

DAY 29
ACTIVATING KINDNESS

A Word with God – *Lectio Divina*

LECTIO
(READ)

Read **Luke 6:32-36** slowly, then read it again. Read it a third time. Look for details. Notice key words, verbs and nouns, and anything repeated, compared, or contrasted.

MEDITATIO
(MEDITATE)

Mentally "chew" on the passage's key words or images to extract their meaning. Let the words sink in and take hold. What words or phrases catch and hold your attention?

_____

_____

_____

_____

_____

_____

_____

ORATIO
(PRAY)

Pay attention to the way your meditation connects with your life, and respond to what you find. This is your time to "have a word" with God through his Word! Speak to him in your words. Make it personal. Share your heart: He is listening.

CONTEMPLATIO
(CONTEMPLATE)

Savor being in God's presence. Enjoy what God has given you.

IMITATIO
(IMITATE)

Resolve to act on what God has revealed to you in *lectio divina*. Recall the characteristics of a disciple at the focus of today's Scripture verses. What specific attitude or action of a disciple will you imitate?

_____

_____

_____

_____

_____

_____

A WORD OF ENCOURAGEMENT

"Kindness is like surprising someone with the love of God. They weren't expecting it, but they needed it. Kindness opens hearts that are closed and grabs the attention of those who are indifferent to the gospel."

— *Jeff Cavins*

Situational Awareness

Note circumstances during your day that gave you the opportunity to exercise the characteristic of a disciple that God revealed to you in your time with him.

_____

_____

_____

_____

_____

_____

_____

_____

_____

_____

_____

Check-In

Cultivate your ongoing relationship with your saintly posse daily, and work with your accountability partner once a week to discuss your walk with Christ.

☐ Today I checked in with my posse.

☐ Today I checked in with my accountability partner.

The Shape of My Day

1. Express Gratitude: Give thanks to God for the gifts he has given you today.

Today I give thanks for _____

_____

_____

_____

2. Seek Grace: Ask God for the insight to see what he's been trying to reveal to you throughout the day, and for guidance in recognizing the hurdles you faced in trying to do his will.

Lord, grant me the grace today to _____

_____

_____

_____

_____

3. Review the Day: Review the day you just lived like a film in your head, paying close attention to moments you felt close to God, those in which you did not, and how you chose to respond in these moments. Then talk to the Lord; share your heart.

Lord, I felt close to you today when _____

_____

_____

_____

_____

4. Ask for Forgiveness: Admit any mistakes you made today and ask God to heal your heart.

Today, Lord, I ask forgiveness for _____

_____

_____

_____

_____

5. Look Forward: Take the insights God has given you today and ask him where he is leading you. What does he want from you tomorrow? Together, in relationship with him and through his grace, prepare yourself to take on the next day.

Today I experienced _____

_____

_____

_____

_____

Tomorrow I am going to focus on _____

_____

_____

_____

_____

☐ *I Lived Day 29 as an Activated Disciple!*

DAY 30
ACTIVATING KINDNESS

A Word with God – *Lectio Divina*

LECTIO
(READ)

Read **Matthew 14:13-16** slowly, then read it again. Read it a third time. Look for details. Notice key words, verbs and nouns, and anything repeated, compared, or contrasted.

MEDITATIO
(MEDITATE)

Mentally "chew" on the passage's key words or images to extract their meaning. Let the words sink in and take hold. What words or phrases catch and hold your attention?

_____

_____

_____

_____

_____

_____

_____

ORATIO
(PRAY)

Pay attention to the way your meditation connects with your life, and respond to what you find. This is your time to "have a word" with God through his Word! Speak to him in your words. Make it personal. Share your heart: He is listening.

CONTEMPLATIO
(CONTEMPLATE)

Savor being in God's presence. Enjoy what God has given you.

IMITATIO
(IMITATE)

Resolve to act on what God has revealed to you in *lectio divina.* Recall the characteristics of a disciple at the focus of today's Scripture verses. What specific attitude or action of a disciple will you imitate?

_____

_____

_____

_____

_____

_____

A WORD OF ENCOURAGEMENT

"Back in 1982, I did not have much money. One Sunday, I opened my Bible and there between the pages was a one-hundred-dollar bill. My heart leapt for joy—we really needed it! Someone demonstrated kindness by giving us a gift. Whoever you were, thanks!"

— *Jeff Cavins*

Situational Awareness

Note circumstances during your day that gave you the opportunity to exercise the characteristic of a disciple that God revealed to you in your time with him.

_____

_____

_____

_____

_____

_____

_____

_____

_____

Check-In

Cultivate your ongoing relationship with your saintly posse daily, and work with your accountability partner once a week to discuss your walk with Christ.

☐ Today I checked in with my posse.

☐ Today I checked in with my accountability partner.

The Shape of My Day

1. Express Gratitude: Give thanks to God for the gifts he has given you today.

Today I give thanks for _____

_____

_____

_____

2. Seek Grace: Ask God for the insight to see what he's been trying to reveal to you throughout the day, and for guidance in recognizing the hurdles you faced in trying to do his will.

Lord, grant me the grace today to _____

_____

_____

_____

_____

3. Review the Day: Review the day you just lived like a film in your head, paying close attention to moments you felt close to God, those in which you did not, and how you chose to respond in these moments. Then talk to the Lord; share your heart.

Lord, I felt close to you today when _____

_____

_____

_____

_____

4. Ask for Forgiveness: Admit any mistakes you made today and ask God to heal your heart.

Today, Lord, I ask forgiveness for _____

_____

_____

_____

_____

5. Look Forward: Take the insights God has given you today and ask him where he is leading you. What does he want from you tomorrow? Together, in relationship with him and through his grace, prepare yourself to take on the next day.

Today I experienced _____

_____

_____

_____

_____

Tomorrow I am going to focus on _____

_____

_____

_____

_____

☐ *I Lived Day 30 as an Activated Disciple!*

" Since you cannot do good to all,
you are to pay special attention to those
who, by the accidents of time, or place,
or circumstances, are brought into
closer connection with you. *"*

— *St. Augustine of Hippo*

ATTENTIVENESS

Sometimes life seems like a blur. Day in and day out, we go through the same routines and can find ourselves bored with life. Is there a way to see every day as a new adventure with Christ? The answer is yes, and one key is to begin to notice the details of each day. In other words, become attentive to the life around you.

For the activated disciple, every day comes with opportunities to serve, love, and introduce others to Christ. These opportunities fly by us if we aren't looking for them, so we must begin to live with a new, heightened sense of awareness, a supernatural attentiveness.

At home, at work, and among acquaintances, be aware of what you are seeing and what you are hearing, all the while listening to the Lord as a disciple. You will often notice opportunities to love and serve as an extension of Christ.

Jesus was very aware of the details around him, and he knew when people were wanting something from him. We see an example of his attentiveness in Luke 8. A woman who had suffered with a flow of blood for twelve years reached out and touched the fringe of Jesus' garment and was instantly healed. At that moment Jesus asked, "Who was it that touched me?" It seemed like a funny question, given how many people were pressing upon him in the crowd, but he felt something when she made contact with him.

Jesus was attentive to the needs of others and was aware that they were pulling on him for attention. How many times in your life do others give clues that they are hurting or have a need that you could address?

One phrase that describes the attentiveness of a disciple is "situational awareness." Wherever you go, be aware of your

surroundings and the needs that might pop up. It could be at church, a restaurant, or the fitness club. God is very capable of setting you up with someone who needs to hear from him.

Attentiveness begins with you. We are called to be attentive to God's Word during Mass. The *Catechism* tells us, "The dignity of the Word of God requires the church to have a suitable place for announcing his message so that the attention of the people may be easily directed to that place during the liturgy of the Word" (CCC 1184).

Attentiveness extends to your family. Many times we focus on work and friends but fail to be attentive to our own spouse, children, or parents. As a disciple, we must pay attention to the spiritual and practical needs of our own families. The family is a school of love, and class is always in session. Be present.

Attentiveness goes beyond our prayer time and our family and extends to society as well. When you see a need that you can address or an act of kindness that is needed, courageously embrace the opportunity and respond as a representative of Jesus.

Finally, not only must we be attentive to the opportunities of the day, but we must be attentive to the Holy Spirit and what he is trying to accomplish in our lives. This is why the Examen prayer is so important at the end of the day. When God wants to review your day, it would be good to have some memory of how your day unfolded.

TALMIDIM CHALLENGE

- Notice the themes in your thoughts that recur throughout the day. Maybe God is trying to say something to you.

- Before going to Mass this week, prepare yourself to be disciplined in hearing the Word proclaimed. Don't allow your mind to drift when God speaks to you from Scripture.

- On the way to work or on your way home, ask the Lord to open your eyes to the needs of others, needs that you may be able to do something about. Look for the details in the faces of others and their tone of voice.

DAY 31

ACTIVATING ATTENTIVENESS

☐ Watch video: Attentiveness, Part 1

A Word with God – *Lectio Divina*

LECTIO
(READ)

Read **Matthew 25:1-13** slowly, then read it again. Read it a third time. Look for details. Notice key words, verbs and nouns, and anything repeated, compared, or contrasted.

MEDITATIO
(MEDITATE)

Mentally "chew" on the passage's key words or images to extract their meaning. Let the words sink in and take hold. What words or phrases catch and hold your attention?

_____

_____

_____

_____

_____

_____

_____

_____

ORATIO
(PRAY)

Pay attention to the way your meditation connects with your life, and respond to what you find. This is your time to "have a word" with God through his Word! Speak to him in your words. Make it personal. Share your heart: He is listening.

CONTEMPLATIO
(CONTEMPLATE)

Savor being in God's presence. Enjoy what God has given you.

IMITATIO
(IMITATE)

Resolve to act on what God has revealed to you in *lectio divina*. Recall the characteristics of a disciple at the focus of today's Scripture verses. What specific attitude or action of a disciple will you imitate?

_____

_____

_____

_____

_____

_____

A WORD OF ENCOURAGEMENT

"Remember that an activated disciple is someone who anticipates divine encounters. Today, prepare your heart for pre-arranged appointments with those whom God wants you to meet. Be alert, ready, and prepared to share the reason for the joy in your heart!"

— *Jeff Cavins*

Situational Awareness

Note circumstances during your day that gave you the opportunity to exercise the characteristic of a disciple that God revealed to you in your time with him.

_____

_____

_____

_____

_____

_____

_____

_____

_____

_____

Check-In

Cultivate your ongoing relationship with your saintly posse daily, and work with your accountability partner once a week to discuss your walk with Christ.

☐ Today I checked in with my posse.

☐ Today I checked in with my accountability partner.

The Shape of My Day

1. Express Gratitude: Give thanks to God for the gifts he has given you today.

Today I give thanks for _____

_____

_____

_____

2. Seek Grace: Ask God for the insight to see what he's been trying to reveal to you throughout the day, and for guidance in recognizing the hurdles you faced in trying to do his will.

Lord, grant me the grace today to _____

_____

_____

_____

3. Review the Day: Review the day you just lived like a film in your head, paying close attention to moments you felt close to God, those in which you did not, and how you chose to respond in these moments. Then talk to the Lord; share your heart.

Lord, I felt close to you today when _____

_____

_____

_____

_____

4. Ask for Forgiveness: Admit any mistakes you made today and ask God to heal your heart.

Today, Lord, I ask forgiveness for _____

_____

_____

_____

_____

5. Look Forward: Take the insights God has given you today and ask him where he is leading you. What does he want from you tomorrow? Together, in relationship with him and through his grace, prepare yourself to take on the next day.

Today I experienced _____

_____

_____

_____

_____

Tomorrow I am going to focus on _____

_____

_____

_____

_____

☐ *I Lived Day 31 as an Activated Disciple!*

DAY 32
ACTIVATING ATTENTIVENESS

A Word with God – *Lectio Divina*

LECTIO
(READ)

Read **Deuteronomy 11:18-21** slowly, then read it again. Read it a third time. Look for details. Notice key words, verbs and nouns, and anything repeated, compared, or contrasted.

MEDITATIO
(MEDITATE)

Mentally "chew" on the passage's key words or images to extract their meaning. Let the words sink in and take hold. What words or phrases catch and hold your attention?

_____

_____

_____

_____

_____

_____

_____

_____

ORATIO
(PRAY)

Pay attention to the way your meditation connects with your life, and respond to what you find. This is your time to "have a word" with God through his Word! Speak to him in your words. Make it personal. Share your heart: He is listening.

CONTEMPLATIO
(CONTEMPLATE)

Savor being in God's presence. Enjoy what God has given you.

IMITATIO
(IMITATE)

Resolve to act on what God has revealed to you in *lectio divina*. Recall the characteristics of a disciple at the focus of today's Scripture verses. What specific attitude or action of a disciple will you imitate?

_____

_____

_____

_____

_____

_____

A WORD OF ENCOURAGEMENT

"There is so much pressure today to succeed and make a name for yourself in the world. However, attentiveness to things at home pays a big dividend in the kingdom of God. May we always remember, there's no place like home!"

— *Jeff Cavins*

Situational Awareness

Note circumstances during your day that gave you the opportunity to exercise the characteristic of a disciple that God revealed to you in your time with him.

_____

_____

_____

_____

_____

_____

_____

_____

_____

_____

Check-In

Cultivate your ongoing relationship with your saintly posse daily, and work with your accountability partner once a week to discuss your walk with Christ.

☐ Today I checked in with my posse.

☐ Today I checked in with my accountability partner.

The Shape of My Day

1. Express Gratitude: Give thanks to God for the gifts he has given you today.

Today I give thanks for _____

_____

_____

_____

2. Seek Grace: Ask God for the insight to see what he's been trying to reveal to you throughout the day, and for guidance in recognizing the hurdles you faced in trying to do his will.

Lord, grant me the grace today to _____

_____

_____

_____

3. Review the Day: Review the day you just lived like a film in your head, paying close attention to moments you felt close to God, those in which you did not, and how you chose to respond in these moments. Then talk to the Lord; share your heart.

Lord, I felt close to you today when _____

_____

_____

_____

_____

4. Ask for Forgiveness: Admit any mistakes you made today and ask God to heal your heart.

Today, Lord, I ask forgiveness for _____

_____

_____

_____

5. Look Forward: Take the insights God has given you today and ask him where he is leading you. What does he want from you tomorrow? Together, in relationship with him and through his grace, prepare yourself to take on the next day.

Today I experienced _____

_____

_____

_____

Tomorrow I am going to focus on _____

_____

_____

_____

☐ *I Lived Day 32 as an Activated Disciple!*

DAY 33

ACTIVATING ATTENTIVENESS

☐ Watch video: Attentiveness, Part 2

A Word with God – *Lectio Divina*

LECTIO
(READ)

Read **Luke 7:36-39 and 7:44-50** slowly, then read it again. Read it a third time. Look for details. Notice key words, verbs and nouns, and anything repeated, compared, or contrasted.

MEDITATIO
(MEDITATE)

Mentally "chew" on the passage's key words or images to extract their meaning. Let the words sink in and take hold. What words or phrases catch and hold your attention?

_____

_____

_____

_____

_____

_____

_____

_____

ORATIO
(PRAY)

Pay attention to the way your meditation connects with your life, and respond to what you find. This is your time to "have a word" with God through his Word! Speak to him in your words. Make it personal. Share your heart: He is listening.

CONTEMPLATIO
(CONTEMPLATE)

Savor being in God's presence. Enjoy what God has given you.

IMITATIO
(IMITATE)

Resolve to act on what God has revealed to you in *lectio divina*. Recall the characteristics of a disciple at the focus of today's Scripture verses. What specific attitude or action of a disciple will you imitate?

_____

_____

_____

_____

_____

_____

A WORD OF ENCOURAGEMENT

"Do you sometimes find that you can go days without really worshipping the Lord? I know we think about him and maybe even say a brief prayer, but when was the last time you purposely went to Adoration and just plain worshipped Jesus. This is attentiveness!"

— *Jeff Cavins*

Situational Awareness

Note circumstances during your day that gave you the opportunity to exercise the characteristic of a disciple that God revealed to you in your time with him.

_____

_____

_____

_____

_____

_____

_____

_____

_____

_____

_____

Check-In

Cultivate your ongoing relationship with your saintly posse daily, and work with your accountability partner once a week to discuss your walk with Christ.

☐ Today I checked in with my posse.

☐ Today I checked in with my accountability partner.

The Shape of My Day

1. Express Gratitude: Give thanks to God for the gifts he has given you today.

Today I give thanks for _____

_____

_____

_____

2. Seek Grace: Ask God for the insight to see what he's been trying to reveal to you throughout the day, and for guidance in recognizing the hurdles you faced in trying to do his will.

Lord, grant me the grace today to _____

_____

_____

_____

_____

3. Review the Day: Review the day you just lived like a film in your head, paying close attention to moments you felt close to God, those in which you did not, and how you chose to respond in these moments. Then talk to the Lord; share your heart.

Lord, I felt close to you today when _____

_____

_____

_____

_____

4. **Ask for Forgiveness:** Admit any mistakes you made today and ask God to heal your heart.

Today, Lord, I ask forgiveness for _____

_____

_____

_____

_____

5. **Look Forward:** Take the insights God has given you today and ask him where he is leading you. What does he want from you tomorrow? Together, in relationship with him and through his grace, prepare yourself to take on the next day.

Today I experienced _____

_____

_____

_____

_____

Tomorrow I am going to focus on _____

_____

_____

_____

_____

☐ *I Lived Day 33 as an Activated Disciple!*

DAY 34
ACTIVATING ATTENTIVENESS

A Word with God – *Lectio Divina*

LECTIO
(READ)

Read **Romans 12:3-8** slowly, then read it again. Read it a third time. Look for details. Notice key words, verbs and nouns, and anything repeated, compared, or contrasted.

MEDITATIO
(MEDITATE)

Mentally "chew" on the passage's key words or images to extract their meaning. Let the words sink in and take hold. What words or phrases catch and hold your attention?

_____

_____

_____

_____

_____

_____

_____

_____

ORATIO
(PRAY)

Pay attention to the way your meditation connects with your life, and respond to what you find. This is your time to "have a word" with God through his Word! Speak to him in your words. Make it personal. Share your heart: He is listening.

CONTEMPLATIO
(CONTEMPLATE)

Savor being in God's presence. Enjoy what God has given you.

IMITATIO
(IMITATE)

Resolve to act on what God has revealed to you in *lectio divina*. Recall the characteristics of a disciple at the focus of today's Scripture verses. What specific attitude or action of a disciple will you imitate?

_____

_____

_____

_____

_____

_____

A WORD OF ENCOURAGEMENT

"As a result of being a member of the body of Christ, I am more appreciative of the other members of the Church and their gifts. Today, tell one other person how appreciative and blessed you are to have them in your life."

— *Jeff Cavins*

Situational Awareness

Note circumstances during your day that gave you the opportunity to exercise the characteristic of a disciple that God revealed to you in your time with him.

_____

_____

_____

_____

_____

_____

_____

_____

_____

_____

_____

Check-In

Cultivate your ongoing relationship with your saintly posse daily, and work with your accountability partner once a week to discuss your walk with Christ.

☐ Today I checked in with my posse.

☐ Today I checked in with my accountability partner.

The Shape of My Day

1. **Express Gratitude:** Give thanks to God for the gifts he has given you today.

   Today I give thanks for _____

   _____

   _____

   _____

2. **Seek Grace:** Ask God for the insight to see what he's been trying to reveal to you throughout the day, and for guidance in recognizing the hurdles you faced in trying to do his will.

   Lord, grant me the grace today to _____

   _____

   _____

   _____

   _____

3. **Review the Day:** Review the day you just lived like a film in your head, paying close attention to moments you felt close to God, those in which you did not, and how you chose to respond in these moments. Then talk to the Lord; share your heart.

   Lord, I felt close to you today when _____

   _____

   _____

   _____

   _____

4. **Ask for Forgiveness:** Admit any mistakes you made today and ask God to heal your heart.

Today, Lord, I ask forgiveness for _____

_____

_____

_____

_____

5. **Look Forward:** Take the insights God has given you today and ask him where he is leading you. What does he want from you tomorrow? Together, in relationship with him and through his grace, prepare yourself to take on the next day.

Today I experienced _____

_____

_____

_____

Tomorrow I am going to focus on _____

_____

_____

_____

_____

☐ *I Lived Day 34 as an Activated Disciple!*

DAY 35
ACTIVATING ATTENTIVENESS

A Word with God – *Lectio Divina*

LECTIO
(READ)

Read **Matthew 24:42-51** slowly, then read it again. Read it a third time. Look for details. Notice key words, verbs and nouns, and anything repeated, compared, or contrasted.

MEDITATIO
(MEDITATE)

Mentally "chew" on the passage's key words or images to extract their meaning. Let the words sink in and take hold. What words or phrases catch and hold your attention?

_____

_____

_____

_____

_____

_____

_____

_____

ORATIO
(PRAY)

Pay attention to the way your meditation connects with your life, and respond to what you find. This is your time to "have a word" with God through his Word! Speak to him in your words. Make it personal. Share your heart: He is listening.

CONTEMPLATIO
(CONTEMPLATE)

Savor being in God's presence. Enjoy what God has given you.

IMITATIO
(IMITATE)

Resolve to act on what God has revealed to you in *lectio divina.* Recall the characteristics of a disciple at the focus of today's Scripture verses. What specific attitude or action of a disciple will you imitate?

_____

_____

_____

_____

_____

A WORD OF ENCOURAGEMENT

"One thing that has really helped me to be attentive to the Lord is continuously keeping in my heart the end of all things on earth, and that is heaven. Heaven is our goal; deep, eternal communion with Christ is the heart's longing. Be attentive to him with every step you take toward eternity!"

— *Jeff Cavins*

Situational Awareness

Note circumstances during your day that gave you the opportunity to exercise the characteristic of a disciple that God revealed to you in your time with him.

_____

_____

_____

_____

_____

_____

_____

_____

_____

_____

Check-In

Cultivate your ongoing relationship with your saintly posse daily, and work with your accountability partner once a week to discuss your walk with Christ.

☐ Today I checked in with my posse.

☐ Today I checked in with my accountability partner.

The Shape of My Day

1. **Express Gratitude:** Give thanks to God for the gifts he has given you today.

   Today I give thanks for _____

   _____

   _____

   _____

2. **Seek Grace:** Ask God for the insight to see what he's been trying to reveal to you throughout the day, and for guidance in recognizing the hurdles you faced in trying to do his will.

   Lord, grant me the grace today to _____

   _____

   _____

   _____

3. **Review the Day:** Review the day you just lived like a film in your head, paying close attention to moments you felt close to God, those in which you did not, and how you chose to respond in these moments. Then talk to the Lord; share your heart.

   Lord, I felt close to you today when _____

   _____

   _____

   _____

4. Ask for Forgiveness: Admit any mistakes you made today and ask God to heal your heart.

Today, Lord, I ask forgiveness for _____

_____

_____

_____

_____

5. Look Forward: Take the insights God has given you today and ask him where he is leading you. What does he want from you tomorrow? Together, in relationship with him and through his grace, prepare yourself to take on the next day.

Today I experienced _____

_____

_____

_____

_____

Tomorrow I am going to focus on _____

_____

_____

_____

_____

☐ *I Lived Day 35 as an Activated Disciple!*

NOTES

" In the life of the body a man is sometimes sick, and unless he takes medicine, he will die. Even so in the spiritual life a man is sick on account of sin. For that reason, he needs medicine so that he may be restored to health; and this grace is bestowed in the Sacrament of Penance. "

— *St. Thomas Aquinas*

CONTRITION

How does the follower of Jesus maintain a positive, holy, and righteous trajectory toward becoming like him? The answer is to maintain a contrite heart.

For the disciple of Jesus to walk with a contrite heart means that the disciple gives daily attention to the condition of his or her heart. Sin is the enemy of the disciple and the one thing that will hinder or stop spiritual growth. The result of sin when not attended to is a hardened heart. A hardened heart will not permit the seed of God's Word to germinate, grow, and bear fruit. In addition, the hardened heart cannot clearly hear the voice of God, resulting in a disoriented life and lack of joy or purpose.

The *Catechism* describes interior repentance as "a radical reorientation of our whole life, a return, a conversion to God with all our heart, an end of sin, a turning away from evil, with repugnance toward the evil actions we have committed. At the same time it entails the desire and resolution to change one's life, with hope in God's mercy and trust in the help of his grace. This conversion of heart is accompanied by a salutary pain and sadness which the Fathers called *animi cruciatus* (affliction of spirit) and *compunctio cordis* (repentance of heart)" (CCC 1431).

Interior repentance is called contrition. It is a sorrow of the soul and a hatred of the sin committed. It is accompanied by a firm resolve to not commit the sin in the future. This is why we say the "act of contrition" in confession. We leave the sacrament of Reconciliation with the intention that we are going to avoid sinning again and will endeavor to avoid even the near occasion of sin.

The Church distinguishes a twofold hatred of sin: perfect contrition, which rises from the love of God who has been offended, and imperfect contrition, which arises principally from some other motive, such as fear of hell.

The activated disciple must aim toward perfect contrition, sorrow for having offended the heart of God. We must never become comfortable with sin, nor should we go to confession thinking that we can go forth to sin again, knowing that reconciliation is always available down the road. This is presuming on the grace of God and is very dangerous for the soul. Pray for a contrite heart. Ask God to help you keep in mind first the sting of offending him, rather than the personal consequences for yourself. See sin as an enemy that has your eternal life in the crosshairs. The goal is to avoid sin because it is an affront to the work of the Cross on your behalf. Give Jesus the fruit of his suffering by avoiding sin and walking with a contrite heart.

TALMIDIM CHALLENGE

- The word "contrition" implies a breaking of something that has become hardened. What areas of your life do you feel may be hardened toward the Lord? Go to confession and ask the Lord to give you a new heart. Break up the fallow ground! "Sow for yourselves righteousness, reap the fruit of mercy; break up your fallow ground, for it is the time to seek the LORD, that he may come and rain salvation upon you" (Hosea 10:12).

- Pray: *God, draw me to your love and give me a heart that will desire you above all that the world has to offer.*

- Remind yourself each day of two things: (1) the goal of sin is death, your death, and (2) the goal of the cross of Christ is life, your eternal life.

DAY 36

ACTIVATING CONTRITION

☐ Watch video: Contrition, Part 1

A Word with God – *Lectio Divina*

LECTIO
(READ)

Read **Revelation 3:19-21** slowly, then read it again. Read it a third time. Look for details. Notice key words, verbs and nouns, and anything repeated, compared, or contrasted.

MEDITATIO
(MEDITATE)

Mentally "chew" on the passage's key words or images to extract their meaning. Let the words sink in and take hold. What words or phrases catch and hold your attention?

_____

_____

_____

_____

_____

_____

_____

_____

ORATIO
(PRAY)

Pay attention to the way your meditation connects with your life, and respond to what you find. This is your time to "have a word" with God through his Word! Speak to him in your words. Make it personal. Share your heart: He is listening.

CONTEMPLATIO
(CONTEMPLATE)

Savor being in God's presence. Enjoy what God has given you.

IMITATIO
(IMITATE)

Resolve to act on what God has revealed to you in *lectio divina*. Recall the characteristics of a disciple at the focus of today's Scripture verses. What specific attitude or action of a disciple will you imitate?

_____

_____

_____

_____

_____

_____

_____

A WORD OF ENCOURAGEMENT

"As I walk with Jesus day by day, I have become aware that
he is knocking on the door of my heart and inviting me to spend
time with him. Sometimes, to my detriment, I ignore that knock,
but the times that I open the door, I'm never disappointed."

— *Jeff Cavins*

Situational Awareness

Note circumstances during your day that gave you the opportunity to exercise the characteristic of a disciple that God revealed to you in your time with him.

_____

_____

_____

_____

_____

_____

_____

_____

_____

_____

Check-In

Cultivate your ongoing relationship with your saintly posse daily, and work with your accountability partner once a week to discuss your walk with Christ.

☐ Today I checked in with my posse.

☐ Today I checked in with my accountability partner.

The Shape of My Day

1. Express Gratitude: Give thanks to God for the gifts he has given you today.

Today I give thanks for _____

_____

_____

_____

2. Seek Grace: Ask God for the insight to see what he's been trying to reveal to you throughout the day, and for guidance in recognizing the hurdles you faced in trying to do his will.

Lord, grant me the grace today to _____

_____

_____

_____

3. Review the Day: Review the day you just lived like a film in your head, paying close attention to moments you felt close to God, those in which you did not, and how you chose to respond in these moments. Then talk to the Lord; share your heart.

Lord, I felt close to you today when _____

_____

_____

_____

_____

4. Ask for Forgiveness: Admit any mistakes you made today and ask God to heal your heart.

Today, Lord, I ask forgiveness for _____

_____

_____

_____

_____

5. Look Forward: Take the insights God has given you today and ask him where he is leading you. What does he want from you tomorrow? Together, in relationship with him and through his grace, prepare yourself to take on the next day.

Today I experienced _____

_____

_____

_____

Tomorrow I am going to focus on _____

_____

_____

_____

□ *I Lived Day 36 as an Activated Disciple!*

DAY 37

ACTIVATING CONTRITION

A Word with God – *Lectio Divina*

LECTIO
(READ)

Read **Acts 3:17-21** slowly, then read it again. Read it a third time. Look for details. Notice key words, verbs and nouns, and anything repeated, compared, or contrasted.

MEDITATIO
(MEDITATE)

Mentally "chew" on the passage's key words or images to extract their meaning. Let the words sink in and take hold. What words or phrases catch and hold your attention?

_____

_____

_____

_____

_____

_____

_____

ORATIO
(PRAY)

Pay attention to the way your meditation connects with your life, and respond to what you find. This is your time to "have a word" with God through his Word! Speak to him in your words. Make it personal. Share your heart: He is listening.

CONTEMPLATIO
(CONTEMPLATE)

Savor being in God's presence. Enjoy what God has given you.

IMITATIO
(IMITATE)

Resolve to act on what God has revealed to you in *lectio divina*. Recall the characteristics of a disciple at the focus of today's Scripture verses. What specific attitude or action of a disciple will you imitate?

_____

_____

_____

_____

_____

_____

_____

A WORD OF ENCOURAGEMENT

"Nothing destroys the peace of God like sin. Sin's goal is to separate and ultimately alienate us from God. Part of being attentive is monitoring our hearts to make sure that we are walking in righteousness. Be attentive to sin and its results. Be quick to turn away from sin."

— *Jeff Cavins*

Situational Awareness

Note circumstances during your day that gave you the opportunity to exercise the characteristic of a disciple that God revealed to you in your time with him.

_____

_____

_____

_____

_____

_____

_____

_____

_____

_____

Check-In

Cultivate your ongoing relationship with your saintly posse daily, and work with your accountability partner once a week to discuss your walk with Christ.

☐ Today I checked in with my posse.

☐ Today I checked in with my accountability partner.

The Shape of My Day

1. Express Gratitude: Give thanks to God for the gifts he has given you today.

Today I give thanks for _____

_____

_____

_____

2. Seek Grace: Ask God for the insight to see what he's been trying to reveal to you throughout the day, and for guidance in recognizing the hurdles you faced in trying to do his will.

Lord, grant me the grace today to _____

_____

_____

_____

3. Review the Day: Review the day you just lived like a film in your head, paying close attention to moments you felt close to God, those in which you did not, and how you chose to respond in these moments. Then talk to the Lord; share your heart.

Lord, I felt close to you today when _____

_____

_____

_____

_____

4. **Ask for Forgiveness:** Admit any mistakes you made today and ask God to heal your heart.

Today, Lord, I ask forgiveness for _____

_____

_____

_____

_____

5. **Look Forward:** Take the insights God has given you today and ask him where he is leading you. What does he want from you tomorrow? Together, in relationship with him and through his grace, prepare yourself to take on the next day.

Today I experienced _____

_____

_____

_____

Tomorrow I am going to focus on _____

_____

_____

_____

_____

☐ *I Lived Day 37 as an Activated Disciple!*

DAY 38

ACTIVATING CONTRITION

☐ Watch video: Contrition, Part 2

A Word with God – *Lectio Divina*

LECTIO
(READ)

Read **Psalm 51:1-8** slowly, then read it again. Read it a third time. Look for details. Notice key words, verbs and nouns, and anything repeated, compared, or contrasted.

MEDITATIO
(MEDITATE)

Mentally "chew" on the passage's key words or images to extract their meaning. Let the words sink in and take hold. What words or phrases catch and hold your attention?

_____

_____

_____

_____

_____

_____

_____

ORATIO
(PRAY)

Pay attention to the way your meditation connects with your life, and respond to what you find. This is your time to "have a word" with God through his Word! Speak to him in your words. Make it personal. Share your heart: He is listening.

CONTEMPLATIO
(CONTEMPLATE)

Savor being in God's presence. Enjoy what God has given you.

IMITATIO
(IMITATE)

Resolve to act on what God has revealed to you in *lectio divina*. Recall the characteristics of a disciple at the focus of today's Scripture verses. What specific attitude or action of a disciple will you imitate?

_____

_____

_____

_____

_____

_____

_____

A WORD OF ENCOURAGEMENT

"I used to go to confession only when I felt I needed to. Today, I regularly go whether I think I need to or not. When I'm attentive to the sacrament of Reconciliation, I'm always amazed at what shows up in my heart as I examine my conscience."

— *Jeff Cavins*

Situational Awareness

Note circumstances during your day that gave you the opportunity to exercise the characteristic of a disciple that God revealed to you in your time with him.

_____

_____

_____

_____

_____

_____

_____

_____

_____

_____

_____

Check-In

Cultivate your ongoing relationship with your saintly posse daily, and work with your accountability partner once a week to discuss your walk with Christ.

☐ Today I checked in with my posse.

☐ Today I checked in with my accountability partner.

The Shape of My Day

1. **Express Gratitude:** Give thanks to God for the gifts he has given you today.

   Today I give thanks for _____

   _____

   _____

   _____

2. **Seek Grace:** Ask God for the insight to see what he's been trying to reveal to you throughout the day, and for guidance in recognizing the hurdles you faced in trying to do his will.

   Lord, grant me the grace today to _____

   _____

   _____

   _____

   _____

3. **Review the Day:** Review the day you just lived like a film in your head, paying close attention to moments you felt close to God, those in which you did not, and how you chose to respond in these moments. Then talk to the Lord; share your heart.

   Lord, I felt close to you today when _____

   _____

   _____

   _____

   _____

4. Ask for Forgiveness: Admit any mistakes you made today and ask God to heal your heart.

Today, Lord, I ask forgiveness for _____

_____

_____

_____

_____

5. Look Forward: Take the insights God has given you today and ask him where he is leading you. What does he want from you tomorrow? Together, in relationship with him and through his grace, prepare yourself to take on the next day.

Today I experienced _____

_____

_____

_____

_____

Tomorrow I am going to focus on _____

_____

_____

_____

_____

☐ *I Lived Day 38 as an Activated Disciple!*

DAY 39
ACTIVATING CONTRITION

A Word with God – *Lectio Divina*

LECTIO
(READ)

Read **2 Corinthians 7:9-11** slowly, then read it again. Read it a third time. Look for details. Notice key words, verbs and nouns, and anything repeated, compared, or contrasted.

MEDITATIO
(MEDITATE)

Mentally "chew" on the passage's key words or images to extract their meaning. Let the words sink in and take hold. What words or phrases catch and hold your attention?

_____

_____

_____

_____

_____

_____

_____

ORATIO
(PRAY)

Pay attention to the way your meditation connects with your life, and respond to what you find. This is your time to "have a word" with God through his Word! Speak to him in your words. Make it personal. Share your heart: He is listening.

CONTEMPLATIO
(CONTEMPLATE)

Savor being in God's presence. Enjoy what God has given you.

IMITATIO
(IMITATE)

Resolve to act on what God has revealed to you in *lectio divina.* Recall the characteristics of a disciple at the focus of today's Scripture verses. What specific attitude or action of a disciple will you imitate?

_____

_____

_____

_____

_____

_____

A WORD OF ENCOURAGEMENT

"I asked myself the other day, 'Are you bothered over sin because you simply fear hell or are you upset because you have hurt the very one, Christ, who loves you and died for you?' I find that I need to keep praying that I will be sensitive to the Sacred Heart of Jesus."

— *Jeff Cavins*

Situational Awareness

Note circumstances during your day that gave you the opportunity to exercise the characteristic of a disciple that God revealed to you in your time with him.

_____

_____

_____

_____

_____

_____

_____

_____

_____

_____

Check-In

Cultivate your ongoing relationship with your saintly posse daily, and work with your accountability partner once a week to discuss your walk with Christ.

☐ Today I checked in with my posse.

☐ Today I checked in with my accountability partner.

The Shape of My Day

1. **Express Gratitude:** Give thanks to God for the gifts he has given you today.

   Today I give thanks for _____

   _____

   _____

   _____

2. **Seek Grace:** Ask God for the insight to see what he's been trying to reveal to you throughout the day, and for guidance in recognizing the hurdles you faced in trying to do his will.

   Lord, grant me the grace today to _____

   _____

   _____

   _____

3. **Review the Day:** Review the day you just lived like a film in your head, paying close attention to moments you felt close to God, those in which you did not, and how you chose to respond in these moments. Then talk to the Lord; share your heart.

   Lord, I felt close to you today when _____

   _____

   _____

   _____

4. **Ask for Forgiveness:** Admit any mistakes you made today and ask God to heal your heart.

Today, Lord, I ask forgiveness for _____

_____

_____

_____

_____

5. **Look Forward:** Take the insights God has given you today and ask him where he is leading you. What does he want from you tomorrow? Together, in relationship with him and through his grace, prepare yourself to take on the next day.

Today I experienced _____

_____

_____

_____

Tomorrow I am going to focus on _____

_____

_____

_____

_____

□ *I Lived Day 39 as an Activated Disciple!*

DAY 40

ACTIVATING CONTRITION

☐ Watch video: Conclusion

A Word with God – *Lectio Divina*

LECTIO
(READ)

Read **Luke 15:17-24** slowly, then read it again. Read it a third time. Look for details. Notice key words, verbs and nouns, and anything repeated, compared, or contrasted.

MEDITATIO
(MEDITATE)

Mentally "chew" on the passage's key words or images to extract their meaning. Let the words sink in and take hold. What words or phrases catch and hold your attention?

_____

_____

_____

_____

_____

_____

_____

_____

ORATIO
(PRAY)

Pay attention to the way your meditation connects with your life, and respond to what you find. This is your time to "have a word" with God through his Word! Speak to him in your words. Make it personal. Share your heart: He is listening.

CONTEMPLATIO
(CONTEMPLATE)

Savor being in God's presence. Enjoy what God has given you.

IMITATIO
(IMITATE)

Resolve to act on what God has revealed to you in *lectio divina*. Recall the characteristics of a disciple at the focus of today's Scripture verses. What specific attitude or action of a disciple will you imitate?

_____

_____

_____

_____

_____

_____

A WORD OF ENCOURAGEMENT

"The further away I get from the Lord, the more restless I feel. As I look at today's Bible verse, I pray that I will become more aware of the peace that will fill me as I draw close to his heart. Lord, give me a contrite heart."

— Jeff Cavins

Situational Awareness

Note circumstances during your day that gave you the opportunity to exercise the characteristic of a disciple that God revealed to you in your time with him.

_____

_____

_____

_____

_____

_____

_____

_____

_____

_____

Check-In

Cultivate your ongoing relationship with your saintly posse daily, and work with your accountability partner once a week to discuss your walk with Christ.

☐ Today I checked in with my posse.

☐ Today I checked in with my accountability partner.

The Shape of My Day

1. Express Gratitude: Give thanks to God for the gifts he has given you today.

Today I give thanks for _____

_____

_____

_____

2. Seek Grace: Ask God for the insight to see what he's been trying to reveal to you throughout the day, and for guidance in recognizing the hurdles you faced in trying to do his will.

Lord, grant me the grace today to _____

_____

_____

_____

3. Review the Day: Review the day you just lived like a film in your head, paying close attention to moments you felt close to God, those in which you did not, and how you chose to respond in these moments. Then talk to the Lord; share your heart.

Lord, I felt close to you today when _____

_____

_____

_____

4. Ask for Forgiveness: Admit any mistakes you made today and ask God to heal your heart.

Today, Lord, I ask forgiveness for _____

_____

_____

_____

_____

5. Look Forward: Take the insights God has given you today and ask him where he is leading you. What does he want from you tomorrow? Together, in relationship with him and through his grace, prepare yourself to take on the next day.

Today I experienced _____

_____

_____

_____

Tomorrow I am going to focus on _____

_____

_____

_____

_____

☐ *I Lived Day 40 as an Activated Disciple!*

" We are not the sum of our weaknesses and failures; we are the sum of the Father's love for us and our real capacity to become the image of his Son. "

— *St. John Paul II*

REFLECTING ON THE CHALLENGE

Congratulations on becoming an activated disciple! Now that you have completed this forty-day challenge, take a moment to reflect on your experience.

What has God revealed to you about your relationship with him, and in what ways has it changed?

_____

_____

_____

_____

_____

In what ways have you grown as a disciple of Jesus? What opportunities do you now see for sharing the *kerygma*, the Good News, with others?

_____

_____

_____

_____

_____

How has the guidance you received from your saintly posse or accountability partner helped you on your path to holiness?

_____

_____

_____

_____

_____

_____

From this day forward, how will your life look different?

_____

_____

_____

_____

_____

_____

"And, above all, does the shape of your day
reflect that you are in love with Christ?"

— _Jeff Cavins_

PRAYERS

The Memorare

Remember, O most gracious Virgin Mary,
that never was it known
that anyone who fled to thy protection,
implored thy help, or sought thy intercession
was left unaided.
Inspired with this confidence, I fly unto thee,
O Virgin of virgins, my Mother;
to thee do I come, before thee I stand,
sinful and sorrowful.
O Mother of the Word Incarnate,
despise not my petitions,
but in thy mercy, hear and answer me. *Amen.*

Litany of Humility

O Jesus, meek and humble of heart,
make my heart like yours.

From self-will, *deliver me, O Lord*.

From the desire of being esteemed, *deliver me, O Lord*.

From the desire of being loved, *deliver me, O Lord*.

From the desire of being extolled, *deliver me, O Lord*.

From the desire of being honored, *deliver me, O Lord*.

From the desire of being praised, *deliver me, O Lord*.

From the desire of being preferred to others,
deliver me, O Lord.

From the desire of being consulted, *deliver me, O Lord*.

From the desire of being approved, *deliver me, O Lord*.

From the desire to be understood, *deliver me, O Lord*.

From the desire to be visited, *deliver me, O Lord*.

From the fear of being humiliated, *deliver me, O Lord*.

From the fear of being despised, *deliver me, O Lord*.

From the fear of suffering rebukes, *deliver me, O Lord*.

From the fear of being calumniated, *deliver me, O Lord*.

From the fear of being forgotten, *deliver me, O Lord*.

From the fear of being ridiculed, *deliver me, O Lord*.

From the fear of being suspected, *deliver me, O Lord*.

From the fear of being wronged, *deliver me, O Lord*.

From the fear of being abandoned, *deliver me, O Lord*.

From the fear of being refused, *deliver me, O Lord*.

That others may be esteemed more than I,
Lord, grant me the grace to desire it.

That in the opinion of the world, others may increase and
I may decrease, *Lord, grant me the grace to desire it.*

That others may be chosen and I set aside,
Lord, grant me the grace to desire it.

That others may be praised and I go unnoticed,
Lord, grant me the grace to desire it.

That others may be preferred to me in everything,
Lord, grant me the grace to desire it.

That others may become holier than I, provided that I may
become as holy as I should, *Lord, grant me the grace to desire it.*

At being unknown and poor, *Lord, I want to rejoice.*

At being deprived of the natural perfections of body and mind,
Lord, I want to rejoice.

When people do not think of me, *Lord, I want to rejoice.*

When they assign to me the meanest tasks,
Lord, I want to rejoice.

When they do not even deign to make use of me,
Lord, I want to rejoice.

When they never ask my opinion, *Lord, I want to rejoice.*

When they leave me at the lowest place, *Lord, I want to rejoice.*

When they never compliment me, *Lord, I want to rejoice.*

When they blame me in season and out of season,
Lord, I want to rejoice.

Blessed are those who suffer persecution for justice's sake,
for theirs is the kingdom of heaven.

THE **ACTIVATED** DISCIPLE
40-DAY CHALLENGE JOURNAL

About the author

Jeff Cavins is passionate about helping people understand Scripture and become disciples of Jesus Christ. Jeff is best known for creating *The Great Adventure*™ Catholic Bible Learning System, which has helped hundreds of thousands of people engage Scripture in a life-changing way. Jeff's other recent projects include his podcast, "The Jeff Cavins Show," and *The Great Adventure Catholic Bible*.

About the editor

Kelly Wahlquist is a Catholic speaker and author. She is the director of the Archbishop Flynn Catechetical Institute in St. Paul, Minnesota; founder of WINE: Women in the New Evangelization; and a contributor to Catholicmom.com. She is the author of *Created to Relate*, and her latest collaborative books, *Walk in Her Sandals* and *Gaze Upon Jesus*, help women relate to Jesus in the way they were created to—as women.

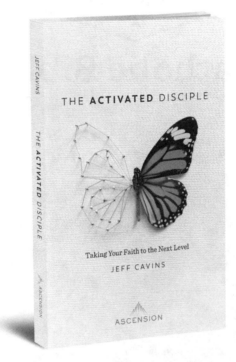

The Catholic Bible That **Teaches You** How to **Read** It

With commentary from the creator of The Great Adventure™, *Jeff Cavins, and renowned Scripture scholars Mary Healy, Andrew Swafford, and Peter Williamson*

The Great Adventure Catholic Bible makes the complexity of reading the Bible simple. The narrative approach gives the big picture of salvation history and shows how everything ties together. This is the only Bible that incorporates *The Great Adventure's* color-coded *Bible Timeline*™ Learning System, a system that has made *The Great Adventure* the most popular and influential Bible study program in the English-speaking world. There has never been another Bible like it!

ascensionpress.com

The Word of **God** **Speaks** to You

Praying Scripture for a Change by Tim Gray

How do you learn to hear God's voice? The key to enriching prayer is an ancient technique known as *lectio divina* ("divine reading"). In this book, Catholic theologian and biblical scholar Dr. Tim Gray walks you through the Bible and the wisdom of the saints to reveal the practical steps of this great treasure of our tradition. The way you pray will be changed forever!

ascensionpress.com